The Object Lessons series achieves something very close to magic: the books take ordinary—even banal—objects and animate them with a rich history of invention, political struggle, science, and popular mythology. Filled with fascinating details and conveyed in sharp, accessible prose, the books make the everyday world come to life. Be warned: once you've read a few of these, you'll start walking around your house, picking up random objects, and musing aloud: 'I wonder what the story is behind this thing?'"

Steven Johnson, author of *Where Good Ideas Come From* and *How We Got to Now*

Object Lessons describe themselves as 'short, beautiful books,' and to that, I'll say, amen. . . . If you read enough Object Lessons books, you'll fill your head with plenty of trivia to amaze and annoy your friends and loved ones—caution recommended on pontificating on the objects surrounding you. More importantly, though . . . they inspire us to take a second look at parts of the everyday that we've taken for granted. These are not so much lessons about the objects themselves, but opportunities for self-reflection and storytelling. They remind us that we are surrounded by a wondrous world, as long as we care to look."

John Warner, *The Chicago Tribune*

T0204905

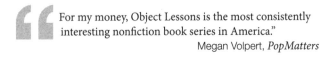

For my money, Object Lessons is the most consistently interesting nonfiction book series in America."

Megan Volpert, *PopMatters*

Besides being beautiful little hand-sized objects themselves, showcasing exceptional writing, the wonder of these books is that they exist at all. . . . Uniformly excellent, engaging, thought-provoking, and informative."

Jennifer Bort Yacovissi,
Washington Independent Review of Books

. . . edifying and entertaining . . . perfect for slipping in a pocket and pulling out when life is on hold."

Sarah Murdoch, *Toronto Star*

[W]itty, thought-provoking, and poetic. . . . These little books are a page-flipper's dream."

John Timpane, *The Philadelphia Inquirer*

Though short, at roughly 25,000 words apiece, these books are anything but slight."

Marina Benjamin, *New Statesman*

"The joy of the series, of reading *Remote Control*, *Golf Ball*, *Driver's License*, *Drone*, *Silence*, *Glass*, *Refrigerator*, *Hotel*, and *Waste* . . . in quick succession, lies in encountering the various turns through which each of their authors has been put by his or her object. . . . The object predominates, sits squarely center stage, directs the action. The object decides the genre, the chronology, and the limits of the study. Accordingly, the author has to take her cue from the *thing* she chose or that chose her. The result is a wonderfully uneven series of books, each one a *thing* unto itself."

Julian Yates, *Los Angeles Review of Books*

"The Object Lessons series has a beautifully simple premise. Each book or essay centers on a specific object. This can be mundane or unexpected, humorous or politically timely. Whatever the subject, these descriptions reveal the rich worlds hidden under the surface of things."

Christine Ro, *Book Riot*

". . . a sensibility somewhere between Roland Barthes and Wes Anderson."

Simon Reynolds, author of *Retromania: Pop Culture's Addiction to Its Own Past*

OBJECTLESSONS

A book series about the hidden lives of ordinary things.

Series Editors:

Ian Bogost and Christopher Schaberg

Advisory Board:

Sara Ahmed, Jane Bennett, Jeffrey Jerome Cohen, Johanna
Drucker, Raiford Guins, Graham Harman, renée hoogland,
Pam Houston, Eileen Joy, Douglas Kahn, Daniel Miller,
Esther Milne, Timothy Morton, Kathleen Stewart, Nigel
Thrift, Rob Walker, Michele White

In association with

BOOKS IN THE SERIES

gin

SHONNA MILLIKEN HUMPHREY

BLOOMSBURY ACADEMIC
NEW YORK • LONDON • OXFORD • NEW DELHI • SYDNEY

BLOOMSBURY ACADEMIC
Bloomsbury Publishing Inc
1385 Broadway, New York, NY 10018, USA
50 Bedford Square, London, WC1B 3DP, UK

BLOOMSBURY, BLOOMSBURY ACADEMIC and the Diana logo are trademarks of
Bloomsbury Publishing Plc

First published in the United States of America 2020

Cover design: Alice Marwick

Bloomsbury Publishing Inc does not have any control over, or responsibility for,
any third-party websites referred to or in this book. All internet addresses given
in this book were correct at the time of going to press. The author and publisher
regret any inconvenience caused if addresses have changed or sites have ceased
to exist, but can accept no responsibility for any such changes.

A catalog record for this book is available from the Library of Congress.

ISBN: PB: 978-1-5013-5327-7
ePDF: 978-1-5013-5329-1
eBook: 978-1-5013-5328-4

Series: Object Lessons

Typeset by Deanta Global Publishing Services, Chennai, India
Printed and bound in the United States of America

To find out more about our authors and books visit www.bloomsbury.com
and sign up for our newsletters.

For Tanya,
with thanks and appreciation.

CONTENTS

1 GIN AND JUICE: AN INTRODUCTION

Gin is, fundamentally, the combination of juniper and any neutral spirit, but depending upon perspective, gin is also grandfathers, Christmas, or sweaty summer nights. Rotten pine needles or raging headaches. Bathtub hooch, speakeasies, British Gin Acts, or Prohibition. Hogarth prints, vintage magazine advertisements, or James Bond. Gin is Snoop Dogg, juniper berries, malaria treatments, seventeenth-century Dutch history, or poured over ice with lime. It is a shortened form of genever (although not really), and with a linguist's eye: cotton seed separating machine, Biblical snare, and a quaint four-person card game.

For me, gin is the first alcohol I tasted.

I was barely sixteen and employed at a small-town movie theater. The general manager, may he now rest in peace, ran a homegrown ammunition factory from the office above the ticket booth. He drank gin from waxed-paper Pepsi cups, and he set up a casual shooting range behind the screen. Before or after our shifts, he sometimes let concession girls fire guns. He sometimes let me drink gin, too.

My first gin Pepsi cup held twenty ounces total: gin from a green bottle mixed with grapefruit juice poured from a large punctured metal can. This was no signature cocktail, crafted with precision. I remember neither the gin nor grapefruit juice brand, but I sipped it with a straw. Before Snoop Dogg popularized the experience, as an employee responsible for the cash register tally at the end of the night, my mind was on the money and the money was on my mind. At age sixteen, however, I was far from laid back as I counted and recounted the bills, trying to remain composed while the dollars seemed to blur and double in my hand.

With some distance now, I am horrified. Who lets a teenager drink gin and shoot guns, even if it was me who begged for the experience? At the time, however, it seemed just fine. Not romantic or illicit or nefarious—just a way to pass a slow work shift. Small-town natives learn early how to make our own fun.

Looking back, those gin Pepsi cups also symbolized a certain freedom. I could not have articulated it then, but it is as clear as a Gilbey's bottle now. Those gin-filled Pepsi cups were lawless, exciting, and provided escape. In a rural, isolated community with narrowly defined gender roles, my gin Pepsi cups seemed innocuous enough at the time, but as an adult, I can see the transgression: young ladies did not sip alcohol on the job. Nice teenaged girls did not shoot guns. Eccentric old men who pack ammunition for fun and provide liquor to minors are bad.

Except, sometimes young ladies did sip alcohol on the job. Sometimes nice teenaged girls did shoot guns. And, sometimes for local boogeymen, scary reputations only carry currency within small-town borders.

More than any other early life experience, I suppose, those early gin Pepsi cups prepared me to tackle questionable—but fun—circumstances later on.

Gin did not improve my target aim, but it did imprint on my palate. With nothing to compare, I grew up believing gin is what liquor should taste like, and I judged each subsequent beverage by a gin standard.

That first Pepsi cup led to other gin drinks. There was a period of Tom Collins orders at the dance club just across the Canadian border in the pre-9/11 era when rural border crossing was nearly as simple as waving hello to the officer sitting in the booth. With gin as my only reference and believing it to be a sophisticated choice, I sipped the cocktail from narrow glasses while dancing on a lighted disco floor to synthesized pop-country songs. The drinking age was nineteen in New Brunswick, and I was probably seventeen at the time.

As a teenager, I had no idea about gin's role in the evolution of the modern cocktail nor did I understand any of gin's broader cultural implications. I did not know that notorious Jazz Age bank robber John Dillinger's favorite drink was supposedly a Gin Fizz, or that Beat writer legend William S. Burroughs killed his wife, fellow Beat writer legend Joan Vollmer, by trying to shoot a gin glass from her head, William Tell–style, at a party in Mexico.

I only knew a Tom Collins tasted like lemonade, and the slender glass felt elegant. After two, my neck felt warm and the sharp edges of perception softened.

Right now, as a woman with an income, a mortgage, and a life spent with ordinary days, I know more about gin's history than I ever imagined. Because my husband gifted me a first-edition copy of Sherwood Anderson's *Hello Towns*, prompting me to learn more about the author, I knew early that Anderson died after swallowing a toothpick, supposedly from his Martini olive, but during this book's research I also learned four main theories about the origin of the Martini. I now know gin is responsible for the earliest vending machine, and this early vending machine was constructed in the shape of a cat. I know gin's history stretches all the way back to alcohol's distillation in AD 100 when a scientist named Maria the Jewess was searching for a chemical path to eternal life.

Once I started seeing gin's placement, it became impossible to cease seeing gin—or its influence—in nearly every aspect of contemporary life. Because of this, I strongly believe gin is much like the six degrees of separation parlor game that connects actor Kevin Bacon to anything in the known universe. Gin and its influence are everywhere.

During a recent trip to New York, gin appeared in the lobby of the Richard Rogers Theater in the form of a specialty intermission cocktail, as well as an order for a Gin and Tonic from the man seated in the airplane row behind me on the return trip home. I heard gin in the lyrics of an

Ed Sheeran song in the taxi and saw anti-gin Hogarth prints when searching the Metropolitan Museum of Art's collection online.

And this was just a weekend of travel.

My work with a family planning clinic taught me that gin, along with a hot bath, was once touted as a reliable abortifacient. Scanning through the 1990s XM radio channel, the Gin Blossoms appeared on the screen. Looking online for a Downton Abbey–themed gift for a friend, I saw that Highclere Castle now brands itself on a gin bottle.

While waiting in line at the Chipotle fast food chain, I looked up nutrition information and learned that juniper flavors the carnitas. At the Starbucks drive through, I noted a juniper latte. When served ceviche from a conical glass on a plate of tortilla chips at an upscale restaurant, I knew that particular shape of stemware likely had gin to thank for its design. From a linguistic standpoint, I see the three-letter g-i-n sequence each time I refer to my red-haired husband as a ginger.

Gin exists everywhere.

Whatever I now understand about gin's impact, my consumption intention has not changed from those teenaged Tom Collins orders. I still drink gin because of its efficiency and how, after two, my neck still feels warm and perception edges still soften. I suspect this is true for most gin drinkers. Gin is efficient, and it works quick. Algonquin Round Table wit and legend Dorothy Parker was correct when she supposedly claimed, "I like to have a Martini, two at the very most; three, I'm under the table, four I'm under my host."

Gin's popularity has risen and fallen throughout history, and my interest, too, fell for a stretch of time. Wine coolers came into fashion, along with Zima, whiskey shots, schnapps, cinnamon liqueur, rum, tequila, beer, and one epic vodka winter picnic that permanently put me off that particular spirit after a friend fished my woozy head from a grubby toilet bowl. There was abstinence, and then a long, long foray into wine: studying it, drinking it, and selling it.

At the time of this book, I have returned to gin: not to youthful and illicit paper Pepsi cups, but to the middle-aged clichés of backyard Gin and Tonic tumblers. I do not mind. In fact, the more I learn about gin, the more I appreciate its simple comfort. In addition to efficient, a Gin and Tonic is direct. A Gin and Tonic is consistent.

Full disclosure: even with the contemporary gin rise, full of unique botanical combinations and small batches lovingly crafted to expand new ways for gin to look, smell, and taste—I prefer the familiar juniper scent of a London Dry with a bottle of tonic (or, if I am honest, any fizzy water from a can, plastic bottle, or soda machine) along with lime or lemon, sliced and squeezed over ice.

Rather than in a music-thumping dance club or hidden behind a soft drink logo in a waxed paper cup, I now enjoy gin from the comfort of a metal glider meant to mimic the look and feel of lawn furniture from the 1950s. It is teal, situated just down the granite garden steps, in front of the sour cherry trees. The glider provides a gentle motion, and the nearby tin tray with a painted rooster pattern (found at a yard sale during a lazy Saturday morning) steadies glasses and pitchers. I like the tinkle of ice cubes and how the scent of lime lingers on my fingertips after squeezing the rind. On hot summer nights, the solar footlights make a lovely reflection.

Gin is, in many ways, how I see myself: comfortable, but evolving. Content. Given the rise of millennial interest in contemporary craft gins, I cannot claim gin is exclusively the drink of the middle aged. Not exactly. Gin has always interested a younger generation of drinker, as well as commitment from the older crowd, while maintaining a reputation among the middle aged. It is unique that way.

Gin possesses a history and a tradition that moves far beyond any hip new discovery. Still, gin is perpetually being rediscovered and reinvented. I did not know this when I was slipping across the Canadian border to meet boys, but I know this now from the comfort of my garden glider. It passes for wisdom.

Gin moves in cycles. Popular, and then not at all. Everywhere, then illicit behind a British Gin Act or Speakeasy door. Replaced by vodka for a period, and then re-made with new flavors, gin is now experiencing an upswing in interest. It will likely swing in the other direction. This pendulum is a loose metaphor for maturity and growth when I think too hard (or drink too much gin), but for now, gin is the beverage where I began and the beverage to which I have returned.

That is the spirit in which I approached this Object Lesson—a settled observer, comfortable in her teal backyard glider. And here is where I claim that while I possess a measure of storytelling skill, I am no gin expert. I neither create it, nor have I spent a lifetime studying it. Because of this, for the technical pieces, I drew heavily from the research and expertise of others: particularly Richard Barnett's *The Book of Gin* (Bloomsbury, 2016), Geraldine Coates's *Gin: The Essential Guide for Gin Aficionados* (Carlton Books, 2019), *Gin: A Global History* (Reaktion Books, 2012) by Lesley Jacobs Solmonson, and David T. Smith's *The Gin Dictionary* (Octopus Publishing Group, 2018). I recommend each of these books wholeheartedly, as well as the excellent— although occasionally contradictory—websites: Gintime. com, Ginfoundry.com, Theginisin.com, Diffordsguide.com, Distillerytrail.com, Sipsmith.com, and Vinepair.com. Every gin question you may have is likely addressed in these resources, and if you contact some of them as blindly as I did, they might offer the same kind responses.

Researching gin and its history, impact, and cultural implications was very much like falling into Alice's Wonderland rabbit hole. One fact led to another that inevitably led to an archive of images, anecdotes, scholarly work, questionable claims, and newspaper articles. For every gin reference, there were a dozen stories or interpretations. A song lyric might lead to an artist interview that cited a poem that contained a reference to a product that had its own historical connections to a crime that was reported with photographs, and I spent hours scrolling through linked images at the Library of Congress website archive.

Stacks of books began to pile on my desk, and twenty tabs stayed open on my internet browser at any given time. Every day, it seemed I was reading a new article about gin or its influence.

I cited fun facts to my parents and co-workers. I reached out to strangers who had written or studied gin more extensively than me. My kitchen smelled like the bottom of a Tanqueray bottle for a weekend while I attempted rhubarb and juniper jam. A friend, while on a holiday, sent me an antique pottery genever cask. I spent more than one early morning paging through online Old Bailey criminal records from the eighteenth century.

My husband stepped in and said, "enough" when I asked him to listen as I read aloud a passage describing a diary kept by Samuel Pepys in the 1600s that detailed his use of a proto-gin as a cure for constipation. I conceded that I'd officially traveled too far down the rabbit hole and acknowledged that not every reader might be as excited as me to learn about a seventeenth-century British naval administrator's flatulence.

(I included it anyway.)

When my husband asked if the book would be boring, I realized that to honestly answer "no," there were hundreds of impossible editorial decisions to make. While describing the etymology of the word and its homonyms, did I mention the role of the cotton gin in the buildup of industry in the southern United States? In the civil rights–era lynching of Emmett Till? What about the Geneva Bible or the different variations of "ginning up"?

In the chapter about lyrics and verse, which of the dozen Prohibition-era songs merited inclusion—only those with gin in the lyrics or instrumentals with gin-based titles, too? Are movies containing culturally significant gin lines, but adapted from books, listed as film or literary references? And, given gin's defining characteristic of juniper, where to draw the line between gin and juniper? Donovan songs? Recipes? What happens when I found lyrics that referred to gin, but also included offensive or degrading language?

Humphrey Bogart's character in *The African Queen*—itself an interpretation of C. S. Forester's novel—is a gin enthusiast, but is that reference best noted as literature and film, or as product placement because of the Gordon's branding that figures prominently on the bottle labels, crates, and the film's advertising posters? It is the same for *The Maltese Falcon* and its bottle of clearly visible Gordon's gin on Humphrey Bogart's desk.

These decisions are author judgment calls, so please consider this book an addition to the gin conversation, and most certainly not a definitive history. Please also consider it a point in time snapshot. My approach to this Object Lesson is classroom styled, and my hope is that each chapter might provide context, a good story, lesser known facts, and spark a broader conversation about gin's role in culture and identity. As a companion to a bottle or cocktail shaker, it might also make a lovely gift, and that is how I imagine its readers: cozy on a chair (or backyard glider) and ready to hear some stories about the spirit's secret life.

So, settle in. Pour yourself a glass, and let's learn about gin.

2 A POTENT THREE-LETTER ETYMOLOGY

What I take from this is that the British were too drunk to pronounce genever so they abbreviated the word to "gen," which eventually gets anglicized to the word that we use today.

SIMON FORD AS TOLD TO CELINE BOSSART IN "THE COMPLETE AND SLIGHTLY INSANE HISTORY OF GIN" PUBLISHED BY *VINEPAIR*

First, the wonkish etymology. As a three-letter sequence, gin can be a verb, noun, acronym, or conjunction. Two consonants; one vowel. Depending upon the century, geography, and context, the G is hard like grapefruit rind or soft like its juice.

This chapter is for grammar enthusiasts, and I recognize that non-enthusiasts might glaze over. Skip to the next section if you must, but to understand why gin in the Bible differs from gin in the bottle, this linguistic section is important.

Pattern recognition kicks in with words like virgin, ginger, begin, or aubergine, and even among non-linguists it is logical to ask, "why do these words, each containing G-I-N, mean very different things?"

We gin up support, appreciate the inventiveness of Eli Whitney's cotton gin (while remaining horrified by its role in Emmet Till's murder), and play the gin or gin rummy card game with our elder relatives. From some of the earliest days of written record, gin was an abbreviation for "ginnen" that was, itself, short for "beginnen." If you are Australian, gin can be an antiquated, offensive slur that profoundly insults a pre-Colonial woman with Aboriginal genealogy. Centuries ago, gin meant a torture device.

Gin can be a slang conjunction if you live in Appalachia. In computer parlance, the GINsystem is a web-based method for college fraternities and sororities to organize and communicate, the GINsim (Gene Interactive Network simulation) is a tool for the modeling and simulation of genetic regulatory networks, and GIN: the Neurofunctional Imaging Group, helps map the human brain. GIN, the Guidelines International Network and its members, develop effective healthcare practices. If you are a Robert Burns fan, you will remember that his "gin a body meet a body/ comin' thro' the rye" figured prominently in J. D. Salinger's notorious novel.

Rarely, if ever, do three individual letters carry such a variety of meanings and historical context, but most of you readers likely picked up this book to learn about the beverage.

To fully understand the word, beverage or otherwise, it is necessary to understand the broader linguistic context. A very brief and simplistic history is this: the Roman Empire eventually fell, so the classical Latin declensions repeated in high school evolved over centuries to form the basis of all Romance languages, and these languages depended on which land region the Latin speakers inhabited.

Because of this Latin heritage, there are two important words with very different Latin definitions at gin's foundation: ingenium and juniperus. From these two bases, distilled two different varieties of gin. Ingenium is the Latin concept for "innate qualities" and juniperus means "the juniper plant." These two lineages are the crux of linguistic (mis) understanding.

Imagine reading the Job chapter of the King James Bible that notes, "The gin shall take him by the heel, and the robber shall prevail against him." While it may be hilarious to imagine a drunken Biblical figure being rolled for cash after a long night of Gimlets, in this instance, gin means "trap," like a snare or net.

This type of gin roots in "ingenium," and, similarly, when a person is described as ginful, the root is also "ingenium." Ingenium's innate qualities include those synonymous with talent, intelligence, and disposition.

Note that "genius" and "engine" are also associations with "ingenium" in this context. Over time, "ginful" came to signify crafty, guileful, and slightly treacherous. If a person was ginful, that person was sneaky. "Engine" derived from this, too, as a clever invention, and its abbreviation propelled us to gin up support or conjure excitement in a creative manner.

Gins of this type include the machine used for separating seeds from bolls of cotton, but the word also applies to various other historical engines: a machine for driving piles, another for raising weights, torture devices, and a pump moved by rotary sails.

Depending upon context, gin's three-letter sequence holds many meanings, but for most readers of this collection, gin arrives in a bottle and has done so in print since at least 1714. While the juniper-flavored beverage is not nearly the oldest form of the three-letter sequence, for more than 300 years, it is, arguably, the most well established. And gin, the beverage's, linguistic journey is much more straightforward.

Juniperus is the Latin word for juniper, and gin contains juniper. While gin evolved as a shortened form of a juniper-related designation, the modern version of the drink did not start as the crisp and clean-tasting beverage recognized on bar shelves today.

Gin, the drink, originated from both Dutch genever and the French ginevre. (Both countries were considered part of the Low Country region.) Both genever and ginevre track to juniperus because juniper is the key ingredient. Say them out loud and notice how, phonetically, the Dutch and French words could easily diverge from their shared Latin juniper root, according to changes in regional dialect.

In Céline Bossart's *VinePair* feature, "The Complete and Slightly Insane History of Gin," gin expert Simon Ford is mostly correct when he jokes that the British were too drunk to pronounce genever, which is how gin condensed to the monosyllable beverage we know today. A common understanding exists that gin is a contraction of genever, and I can easily imagine the social slurring and impromptu contractions happening throughout centuries until it was just easier to get drunk via a single syllable.

However, gin and genever are very different beverages.

Genever, although juniper flavored, is made with a base of malted grain wine, so genever's characteristics are more similar to a whiskey than a typical London Dry Gin. Genever arrived earlier and carried itself with more deference. If genever was the serious, responsible older child who earned high marks in school, gin evolved as the rebellious younger cousin cutting class and smoking cigarettes in the parking lot.

That noted, gin's prototypes—including genever—also possess a long history of clever wordplay that dates back to the earlier mentions of genever in print. Playwright and satirist Philip Massinger is particularly clever in 1623's *The Duke of Milan*:

An officer preaching of sobriety, lo unlesse he read it in Geneva print, lay him by the heels.

The joke is clear: the only acceptable Geneva is the religiously affiliated one. Geneva refers to the Geneva Bible, a specific translation that ranks as, sort of, the first mass-printed and direct-to-consumer edition, predating the King James version by fifty years. Geneva also refers to a colloquial British iteration of genever, sometimes personified as Madame Geneva.

Notice the triple entendre: bible, snare, and beverage. The wordplay adds another level of depth and humor via the gin-as-a-snare association. The insinuation is that any Geneva will trap a person, and it is best to choose the God-led one.

It is quite funny to word nerds.

But how did genever condense—in liquid and linguistic form—to the contemporary gin recognized on shelves today?

Via a slur and an insult, basically.

Geraldine Coates, editor of the website *Gintime* and author of *Gin: The Essential Guide for Gin Aficionados* (Carlton Books, 2019) explains the first appearance of gin as we know it now, in its three-letter form, in printed material.

Fast forward now to 1714 . . . a time when disreputable distillers made rotgut copies of proper genever that were poisoning the urban poor.

And this is where we find the first recorded use of the word "gin" in a political pamphlet entitled, *The Fable of the Bees, or Private Vices, Publick Benefits* by Bernard Mandeville.

Specifically,

Mandeville writes of "*the infamous liquor, the name of which, derived from Juniper berries in Dutch, is now, by frequent use and the Laconick spirit of the Nation shrunk into a Monosyllable, Intoxicating Gin that charms the unactive, the desperate and the crazy of either Sex . . ."*

Not a very flattering depiction and quite far removed from the sophisticated spirit we know today but there it is—the first known mention in print.

The implication is that this was not wine at dinner or sips of sophisticated cordial. Gin in 1714 was akin to methamphetamine today, or crack cocaine in the 1980s, or reefer madness in the 1960s. Gin as a phrase in 1714 was meant as a slur. Neither the refined genever of yesteryear with production regulated and restrained, nor taken medicinally in the form of juniper flavored "strong water" vials carried in pockets in the way a person today might carry an aspirin or antacid, gin was not even a glamorous line of cocaine that showed up on glittery mirrors at Studio 54. In 1714, gin was akin to the meth smoked on street corners by the prostitute, the delinquent, the criminal, and the poor.

"Intoxicating gin that harms the unactive, the desperate, and the crazy of either sex" in 1714 is important because not only does it establish gin as a beverage distinct from genever, but it also establishes its impact on women, who were not only drinking gin at pace with men, but also feeling social ramifications at a pace that outran men.

Genever was meant for polite company, while gin was cut with sulfuric acid, turpentine, or pepper and sold at a discount to those who were too addicted to care that this low-grade product might leave a drinker blind, crippled, or dead.

Which is how, in the simplest of terms, genever transformed into a distinct substance that became known as gin.

NOTE FOR SIDEBAR:

Some argue that "ginning up" is a derivative of "gingering up" a phrase applied in equine circles to make a horse appear energetic and lively. The etymology of the phrase led me to the learning about the unpleasant process of "feague" or "feaguing" a horse, which is described as energizing a horse, particularly its tail, by placing a piece or ginger, or sometimes a live eel, into the horse's fundament. (Fundament is a polite way of saying "bum.")

NOTE FOR SIDEBAR:

Gin rummy, the card game and another common association with the three-letter sequence, is a bit more polarizing. Some claim the juniperus lineage, given that it possibly evolved from a card game called Whiskey Poker, and some claim the ingenium lineage because it was a game popularized during the Great Depression when people, having less money to spend on entertainment, began hosting clever in-home options.

3 THE BASICS: JUNIPER

Gin contains two elements: neutral spirits and juniper flavor, so in preparation for this book, I ordered juniper berries from different sources, each arriving in small glass spice jars or sealed plastic bags. The berries themselves are dry and hard, about a quarter inch in diameter. Slightly smaller than a wild blueberry, but bigger than a peppercorn, juniper berries are colored dark, indigo blue with a dusty gray sheen. I shook a few into my palm and brought them to my nose. The aroma, a subtle pine, intensified when I pinched a berry between my thumb and forefinger, crushing it flat.

The scent is strong and distinct. It is the same scent when a bottle of gin is opened or a glass is poured, and its odor immediately prompts interest or aversion. Some find it delightful, and others stifle a gag reflex. Unlike other spirits, gin relies not on a particular process or recipe. There is no aging requirement. Compared to whiskey, rum, vodka, and others with a specific recipe and protocol, gin is more (ahem) fluid in scope. The juniper flavor—the single aspect that separates gin from other spirits—is an unusual and often acquired taste.

It takes approximately three tablespoons of juniper berries to flavor a bottle of gin, and because this juniper scent and flavor, at least initially, was the general expectation for what gin should taste and smell like, people became very, very wedded to that profile.

Juniper is also what modern gin makers acknowledge as the chief aversion to gin. I toured distilleries in preparation for this book, and each gin maker stressed the difficulty of the flavor and mimicked the pinched faces of those who declined the free samples.

When people smell it, they often back right up.

But what, exactly, is it? What does juniper, particularly juniper in gin, smell and taste like? Strong, piney, chemical? Yes to each of those aspects, but juniper is more than just those descriptors.

Flavor tops the most difficult concepts to translate into words. Try it. How many ways are there to describe, say, chicken? Tender, juicy, and crispy are physical descriptions, but they rely on sight and touch, not taste.

Salt, sweet, sour, bitter, and most recently umami, are taste categories, but to describe them almost always involves a reference to something else. For instance, lemons taste sour, but the description requires a frame of reference and experience with lemons. Or rhubarb. Or unripe apples. Sugar tastes sweet, but so do honey, stevia, molasses, and maple syrup. And, each of these sweet foods taste very different from each other. Salt tastes salty, like pickles or potato chips, but, again, salt becomes the adjective and not the noun. And scents? Kimchi, sardines, and smoked oysters are fragrant, but also fragrant are lavender tea, cinnamon buns, and peaches.

This is what makes food writing—and gin—both frustrating and brilliant.

Unlike whiskey, gin has no color reference or aging requirements. Unlike Champagne, gin lacks bubbles, fizz, and a required production location. Unlike beer, there is no foam to describe. Gin is most like wine in a sense, given its potential for complexity in execution, but unlike gin, wine requires no central element like juniper. (Most wine is, indeed, made from grapes, but dandelion or strawberry wines are still very much wines.) Unlike vodka, we smell gin before we taste it. Gin can be fussy, and gin can be direct.

Since the only specific flavor requirement for gin is the presence of juniper, juniper becomes the central reference point—but read the tasting notes on any given gin, particularly among contemporary gins, and they (more often than not) describe the long list of other ingredients, not the juniper itself. For traditional gin drinkers, strong juniper taste is an assumption, and for contemporary gin lovers, a challenge to overcome.

Imagine a visitor learning about gin for the first time. Gin tastes sweet, like Old Tom. Or like cucumbers in Hendricks.

Or like coriander in Beefeater, except for when drinking the Beefeater strawberry variety which tastes like strawberry candy. Gin tastes like licorice in Tanqueray, and it tastes like honey in Vermont-based Barr Hill gin. In Ireland's An Dulaman Maritime Gin, gin tastes like seaweed.

Now imagine an advertising executive's job to write materials that accurately describe this juniper-based, cucumber-seaweed-coriander-strawberry candy-licorice-honey product. It is no wonder there is confusion.

The recent popularity of craft gin has introduced hundreds of stylized options that include profiles with fennel, almond, anise, angelica (both roots and seeds), rhubarb, kelp, lemon, orange, cassia, nutmeg, ginger, cubeb berries, and orris, all appearing on the long, long list of other flavors. Some gin recipes use just one or two botanicals while others use several dozen.

Remember that these flavors are not part of specialty mixed cocktails, just the basic ingredient itself—all called gin.

To further complicate the situation, gin's mandatory ingredient and defining flavor is juniper—which, by itself and consumed straight from the spice jar, is a sensory experience that aligns with munching pine needles or floor wax.

After noting juniper's significance to gin, it is also worth noting that any juniper-flavored beverages, to include gin, were, generally speaking, not originally flavored by intention. Juniper flavor, I learned, was more an accident of proximity.

Imagine life as a northern European in the Low Country region—what is now Belgium, Holland, and northern

France—during the fourteenth and fifteenth centuries: it was likely agrarian, hard, and short. Add an intemperate climate that included rain and snow, hot summers, and frigid winters. Distillation, particularly the popular brandewijn (literally, "burnt wine") production, became a way to soften the edges of a brutal existence. Although distilled from wine originally, brandewijn evolved as a way to use excess produce and maximize farm profits from a good harvest year, and "burnt wine" became a general term for all spirits.

The trouble was, brandewijns tasted foul and harsh: think industrial cleaning agents or gasoline. Distillation had yet to be perfected for creating a flavorless base, so Low Country residents needed a way to make their liquor taste better. Juniper berries, growing in abundance and already considered a safe, restorative, medicinal option as well as a flavoring for game meats, were used to soften the chemical taste. Over time, this malted grain beverage evolved into genever. People enjoyed the taste and effect, and its popularity made genever a signature aspect of the regional identity.

According to gin expert Geraldine Coates, "Between 1500 and 1700, distilleries were established in every town and distilling became as distinctly Dutch as cheese-making."

Modern juniper berry exports originate in Germany, Albania, India, China, the United Kingdom, Italy, and Belgium, but juniper has one of the most wide-ranging growth footprints of any plant, and it spans from Alaska, Iceland, and Greenland to Japan and parts of north Africa.

Juniper plants are hardy, and they are relatively immune to harsh temperature.

Berries have been discovered in Egyptian tombs, and ancient Romans apparently used juniper in place of the more expensive and harder to obtain peppercorns to flavor food. Natural medicine enthusiasts smudge homes with juniper to invite clarity of mind and to restore creative energy. Juniper's essential oil is said to treat symptoms that range from sleeplessness to heartburn to cellulite.

However broad its scope, if your home is the United States, juniper is not likely a common food flavor. The Penzeys juniper berry bottle that arrived in my mailbox bore a label that indicated:

> Popular as a seasoning for venison, squab, pheasant, and rabbit. A few juniper berries reduce the wild flavor of these meats and add a pleasant tartness. Often used in Germanic dishes such as sauerbraten, stuffed goose, and beer stews.

Growing up in northern Maine, I often ate venison—colloquially, deer meat—but I do not recall it ever flavored with juniper. Nor do I recall juniper berries among the enormous rack of uniform, glass, dried spice jars in my mother or grandmother's kitchen.

As I educated myself for this book, I found juniper-scented body lotions, room sprays, and some loose-leaf teas, but I was able to locate just two juniper-flavored, non-gin, commercially available food options: Seattle, Washington's DRY soda company makes a juniper berry–flavored soft drink, and global coffee giant Starbucks experimented with a seasonal winter holiday juniper-flavored latte.

That's it.

Contemporary juniper-based recipes exist, but they are largely Scandinavian, British, and Dutch—and decidedly epicurean. Among them: vodka and juniper salt-cured salmon; vanilla, fig, and juniper cake; juniper sea salt chocolate panna cotta; and rhubarb and juniper berry jam.

For a berry with such a worldwide geographic range, juniper recipes are particularly regional, and it was a challenge to locate any ready-made *juniper*-flavored food products.

Conversely, the number of *gin*-flavored food products was staggering; gin-flavored yogurts, truffles, sorbet, macarons, pastilles, chocolate bars, potato chips, fudge, marshmallows, gelatin, cupcakes, and jams can be purchased from online store shelves throughout the world, right now.

For recipes, a quick internet search found dozens and dozens of gin or gin and tonic–flavored recipes from all corners of the globe, fancy and accessible, sweet and savory, popsicles to cucumber pickles.

So many products and recipes focused on the *gin* flavor, while the integral *juniper* was significantly underrepresented. Gin requires juniper as its central element, so I wondered where that flavor line began to blur. It felt like one of those standardized entrance exam logic questions: If all gins

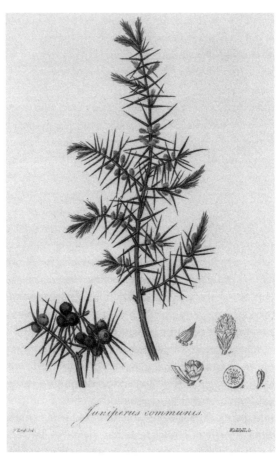

Juniperus communis.

FIGURE 1 Juniperus Communis. 1836. Stephenson, J. and Morss Churchill, J. Medical Botany.

contain juniper, but juniper is not gin, why can I purchase so many gin-flavored products, but almost no juniper products?

While it is easy to create gins that do not taste much like juniper at all, it is difficult—if not impossible—to separate gin from juniper when describing it. I learned this after attempting a recipe for rhubarb/juniper berry jam. A fan of rhubarb, I cut stalks from the patch in my garden. I had high hopes, but results were mixed. My kitchen smelled like an open bottle of gin for a weekend, and the jam itself—while sort of tasty when spread on toast—did give my mouth a medicinal, antiseptic sensation. Licked directly from the spoon, I felt like I had made an error and concocted a sort of rhubarb daiquiri with the jam, but made with gin instead of rum. Not unpleasant, just sweet and very juniper-y.

When speaking about this jam, I reverted to phrases like "tastes like gin" when I meant "tastes like juniper," and I realized how inextricably the two are linked.

NOTE FOR SIDEBAR:

Quick Rhubarb and Juniper Jam

- Approximately 8–10 stalks of rhubarb, chopped
- Approximately 4 cups of sugar
- 1 to 2 teaspoons of dried juniper berries, roughly chopped

Combine all the ingredients in a stock pot. Cook on medium heat until the sugar is dissolved and the jam comes to a boil. Skim the jam to remove any foam. Continue cooking the jam until it reduces and thickens.

Pour into jars and process for longer-term storage or enjoy immediately.

NOTE FOR SIDEBAR:

Juniper berries have many medicinal and spiritual claims, evolving over centuries. Among them, tossing a handful in a bath to invigorate skin or planting near the entrance of a home to ward off evil spirits. Ancient Egyptians used juniper oil to anoint dead bodies. Juniper berries have been used to treat cancer, cure headaches, reduce inflammation in athletes, and limit flatulence. Juniper berries, as well as a series of liquids with juniper added, have been used as medicine since humans began applying botanical solutions to health concerns.

One of the earliest and most widely known references is included in *De Materia Medica*, a five-volume illustrated encyclopedia of plants and their medical uses, written in approximately AD 70. In this book, there is a detailed description of juniper berries steeped in wine and its application as a method to heal a chest cold. It is not exactly gin, but it is an important reference to one of the earliest combinations of juniper and alcohol with an intent to heal.

NOTE FOR SIDEBAR:

A centuries-old folk directive suggests drinking gin and taking a hot bath to end a pregnancy, but it was likely the juniper (and not the gin) acting as abortifacient. Juniper has long been considered harmful to pregnant women.

4 THE BASICS: DISTILLATION

A quick history of distillation is important because distilled spirits are one half of the alcohol + juniper = gin equation, so here is where I mention Maria the Jewess, two Arab scholars, the quest for eternal life, Benedictine monks, the printing press, and one British guy's flatulence. I am, obviously, simplifying a complex scientific evolution from alchemy to medicine to recreational use, as well as the social and religious implications.

First, Maria the Jewess. Although humans were fermenting different foods into wine and beer throughout the world pretty much since recorded time (evidence of a fermented rice, honey, and fruit drink discovered in China apparently dates to 7000–6600 BCE), distillation likely originated and was most definitely advanced in the North African/Middle Eastern region. Alcohol itself is a word with Arabic roots.

The history of distillation is subject to conjecture and supposition, given that so few firsthand accounts exist, but it is generally credited to ancient alchemists as they went hunting for a way to transcend the limits of human and spiritual awareness by attempting to extract a spiritual essence from a body.

One woman and two men are particularly noteworthy.

Maria the Jewess is described as an alchemist who lived at some point between AD 100 and 300 and potentially taught at the University of Alexandria. Variations of her story include iterations of her name (Marie, Miriam, Mary the Prophetess) as well as differing perspectives about her role in Christianity's development, but her scientific advancements set the standard for modern distillation. She is credited with inventing a variety of mechanisms that include a double boiler, the eponymous bain marie, and the prototype for a modern still. Her inventions were unique because they intentionally mimicked the process of distillation in nature, which alchemists believed—if isolated and perfected—would create a path to heaven and ultimate immortality.

Maria is credited with mind-body-spirit-nature alchemical wisdom, such as:

Just as a man is composed of four elements, likewise is copper; and just as a man results from the association of liquids, of solids, and of the spirit, so does copper.

Alchemists believed this process might also, conveniently, transform matter into gold. Although Maria was considered a leader in the field of alchemy, none of her personal writing survives, and we know about Maria primarily through the work of future scholars who regarded her as a sort of long-dead, mythical sage and brilliant scientific mind. Some documents (dubiously) suggest she was a contemporary of Jesus, and psychologist Carl Jung has famously used Maria's phrasing of "join the male and the female, and you will find what is sought," in his work.

From its inception, the process of distillation is credited to an ancient Jewish woman and linked to the quest for immortality and transmutation—a decidedly spiritual endeavor. However, the resulting product, alcohol, had practical healing and social benefits.

It just took a few more centuries to figure that part out.

Enter two Arabic scholars living in AD 800–900: first Abu Musa Jabir Ibn Hayyan (Latinized as Jabir or Geber) and, later, Abu Bakr Muhammed Ibn Zakariyya Al-Razi (Latinized as Rhazes).

I learned that Jabir is largely considered the father of modern chemistry and the man who, through rational process, moved elements of alchemy into a legitimate science. He also perfected distillation. He perfected the process, but he apparently lacked a purpose or market for the result.

So, after Jabir perfected distillation, it was later work by Rhazes, widely recognized by his contemporaries as the greatest physician of the Islamic world, that is credited with alcohol's medicinal use.

Think about that.

Imagine taking an ordinary food like wheat or a potato, grown for nourishment, and by a process of fermentation and heat, transforming that food into a distinct and separate liquid—via spooky smoky vapors—that if consumed, altered a person's state of mind and perception while very often easing (or curing) physical ailments. Or, conversely, prompted uninhibited and sometimes violent behavior from otherwise restrained people.

It was controversial and scary.

It was also how alcohol became the center of a medicine, recreation, spiritual Venn diagram that exists today. Maybe the closest present-day comparison is marijuana, a plant grown and used for centuries with its public response largely dependent on region, religion, medical background, and social politics. Like marijuana, early distilled spirits were sometimes considered a tool of Satan, effective medicine, or a good time—depending upon who was asked. Like marijuana, early distilled spirits were controversial and sparked fear and skepticism, as well as social and political revolt.

In a xenophobic European culture, its Muslim and Jewish roots probably did not help.

However, this much is true: distilled alcohol's uses expanded to include medicinal properties. The distillation process spread to Europe in the Middle Ages from the Arab world via Sicily's Moorish influence, and this spread eventually included a group of Benedictine monks living in southern Italy. These monks recognized alcohol's healing properties, and they also used distilled wines to preserve plants and herbs—among them, again for ease of proximity, the juniper berries that grew nearby in abundance.

This proto-gin mix of juniper berries with wine is described in the circa-1055 publication, *Compendium Salernita*, by the Benedictine monks themselves. (This is how Italy makes a credible claim to gin's invention, centuries before the Dutch figured it out.)

In the eleventh century, distillation expanded to include medicinal use by European scientists and doctors, as well as private efforts in the homes of the wealthy nobility. By the mid-1300s, the Bubonic Plague was raging in full force, and juniper use, as well as juniper-mixed-in-alcohol use, included a kind of perfumed mask-wearing to mitigate the scent of decomposing bodies.

During the Middle Ages, gin's popularity (or, the popularity of elements contained in gin) began to move faster, starting in the 1400s with the introduction of technology.

Specifically, the printing press. This one invention set in motion a chain of widespread impact that lasted for hundreds of years, because printed text became no longer limited to the wealthy upper classes or those studying in a religious order. With the advent of the printing press, knowledge was recorded with the intent to be preserved and shared. This knowledge-sharing included medical books, plant encyclopedias, and household recipe books that contained references to juniper or distillation.

However, even with the invention of the printing press, there was still little in the way of written memoir that detailed the lives of how ordinary people used these distilled proto-gins, as medicine or recreationally, in any given

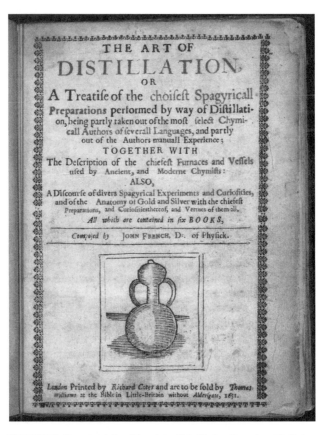

FIGURE 2 French, John. *The Art of Distillation* (London: R. Cotes for T. Williams, 1651).

community. Although the printing press was equalizing access to information during this period, ordinary lives were rarely documented, and extracting information about how gin and its (mis)use impacted the general population was nearly impossible.

This is what makes Samuel Pepys and his diary exceptional. Pepys was a member of British Parliament and a naval administrator, and he kept a personal diary from 1660 to 1669 that has emerged as an important first-person period narrative. In addition to eyewitness accounts of major events like the Plague and Great Fire of London, he also documented one of the earliest everyday medical uses of distilled alcohol: constipation relief.

Consider the diary entry itself:

> Up, and not in any good ease yet, but had pain in making water, and some course. I see I must take besides keeping myself warm to make myself break wind and go freely to stool before I can be well, neither of which I can do yet . . .

Pepys is describing how it hurt to pee, and how he thought he would feel better if he could just pass some gas, but nothing seemed to help. He then told two of his friends, and they both advised him to, basically, drink a little gin.

> I did, however, make shift to go to the office, where we sat, and there Sir J. Minnes and Sir W. Batten did advise me

to take some juniper water, and Sir W. Batten sent to his Lady for some for me, strong water made of juniper.

Pepys specifically describes it as a "strong water made of juniper." At the time, spirits were called "strong waters" or "hot waters" and used regularly as medicine. Although skeptical, Pepys describes some initial success, and then he remains unconvinced.

Whether that or anything else of my draught this morning did it I cannot tell, but I had a couple of stools forced after it . . . but whether I shall grow better upon it I cannot tell.

It is important to remember that Pepys kept his diary from 1660 to 1669, and during this period, these strong water proto-gins were largely only accessible to people who could afford to buy them because production was strictly controlled. Pepys's diary and its clinical reference to "strong water made from juniper" is fairly solid evidence that distilled spirits were predominantly seen as a medicine.

Because Pepys was a respected man with a reputation to uphold, it is unlikely that he would have drank them solely for pleasure—and even had he been inclined to do so, given his reputation, he would have not likely acknowledged it in written form.

NOTE FOR SIDEBAR:

Shortly after his juniper strong water mention, Samuel Pepys also took a moment in his diary to note his wife's poor housekeeping skills.

"Dined at home at noon, my wife and house in the dirtiest pickle that ever she and it was in almost, but in order, I hope, this night to be very clean."

He sounds like a real charmer.

5 CLASS AND TYPE

So, what qualifies as gin? Distilled neutral spirits and juniper flavor.

That's it. Juniper is the sole distinction.

If juniper flavor is present in a neutral spirit, it becomes gin. There is no requirement for how much juniper, in what proportion, or the process for incorporating the juniper flavor. Add juniper berries at the beginning or end of the process, by the bucket or by the spoon, and that juniper flavor makes gin, unless—and this is important—*the liquor qualifies as something else*.

This means that in addition to understanding the (relatively straightforward) elements of gin itself, gin manufacture—particularly manufacture of gins outside the standard London Dry flavor profile—requires a familiarity with other liquor definitions.

As a practical example, consider my visit to a local distiller who explained the process to me. We sat at a table cluttered with stacks of file folders, having just had a lively discussion about bottle shape and color. The former was, he explained, more about hand feel to please bartenders and accommodate refrigerator doors, while the latter included strategy for assuaging panic should any natural sediments settle to the bottom.

This distillery owner also spoke to me about the complications of labeling gin in compliance with federal guidelines. He was excited to introduce a new line of gin that incorporated the flavors and colors resulting from wood barrel storage. However, his approach to gin began with a specific grain and involved oak barrels, and this meant that if he labeled it "barrel aged" as initially planned, the new product must be classified, by definition, as a whiskey—not a gin.

He tipped a clear bottle of the new product onto its side, and with its honey amber hue, it did bear a visual resemblance to whiskey. However, when he removed the cap, it most definitely smelled like juniper.

In the United States, alcohol's oversight is the responsibility of the Department of the Treasury and its Bureaus, specifically the Alcohol and Tobacco Tax and Trade Bureau (TTB). Savvy readers will recognize that Alexander Hamilton was the first Secretary of the Treasury, and it was under his direction that these initial liquor requirements were structured. Savvy readers will also recognize that alcohol's oversight has taken many forms since its inception.

These regulations were initially designed to, among larger moneymaking goals, save lives from unscrupulous vendors selling lethal substances (turpentine, sulfuric acid, and other poisons were often added as cheap ways to simulate gin's chemical taste), and these regulation semantics now ensure a consistent and fair consumer product.

The TTB produces a publication called the Beverage Alcohol Manual (BAM). The BAM prints a section on mandatory labeling information for those wanting to create gin for public sale and consumption, and Chapter 4 details the single quality that differentiates gin from other distilled spirits: juniper's presence in the bottle.

Because of this labeling, gin is defined by what it *is* in equal proportion to what it *is not*. Gin's existence within this negative space is one of the aspects that makes it so fascinating. Think about words like nonfiction, noncommittal, or nondenominational that apply this concept. Gin requires a fundamental grasp of what it does **not** contain, how it is **not** distilled, and the length of time it does **not** age.

Gin is any neutral spirit flavored with juniper, but so many gin profiles and advertising campaigns focus on gin's other flavors and not the juniper itself. This makes writing about gin tricky. Target markets, too, get tricky because if gin is defined in equal proportion by what it is not, that slipperiness also applies to gin drinkers. There is no fixed identity. No single market. No demographic.

In contrast, consider whiskey. From the BAM:

Spirits distilled from a fermented mash of grain . . . having the taste, aroma and characteristics generally attributed to whiskey . . .

These are the elements that define whiskey in its class: *fermented grain with the taste, aroma, and characteristics of whiskey.*

This definition is not especially helpful if a person is unfamiliar with the taste, aroma, or characteristics of whiskey. To assist, there are types of whiskey. The BAM notes forty-one, each with its own unique characteristics and production process, and the more common of these include:

Bourbon Whiskey

Rye Whiskey

Wheat Whiskey

Malt Whiskey

Corn Whiskey

Scotch Whiskey

Irish Whiskey

Canadian Whiskey

For whiskey, each of the 41 types has a definition and these definitions specify the type's ingredients, percentages, and creation process—essentially, what makes each whiskey unique. This system sets a standard and lets whiskey lovers compare different types. For instance, corn whiskey and Irish whiskey.

Corn whiskey is:

Whiskey produced . . . from a fermented mash of not less than 80 percent corn and if stored in oak containers stored . . . in used or uncharred new oak containers and not subjected in any manner to treatment with charred wood.

Compare that to Irish whiskey, which is:

Unblended whiskey manufactured in the Republic of Ireland or in Northern Ireland in compliance with their laws.

It works like this for gin, too, but I emphasize whiskey because unlike whiskey's forty-one types and regional exceptions, gin is its own class, and gin has just three types: distilled, re-distilled, or compound. The BAM notes no geographic distinctions. There is no aging process or particular grain required, no proportion of juniper, and the juniper itself need not be region specific.

Gin's class designation:

Spirits with a main characteristic flavor derived from juniper berries produced by distillation or mixing of spirits with juniper berries and other aromatics or extracts derived from these materials . . .

Gin must involve juniper in some way, and the juniper can be **distilled with** or **added into** neutral spirits made from anything that ferments. This fermentation process strips the flavor, and while some bases get funky (think: beets, carrots, grapes, honey, or sorghum), more common bases include wheat, rye, corn, or potato. Once the base is fermented and distilled, often multiple times to remove as much flavor as possible, juniper makes its appearance—as well as any other botanical herbs and spices.

Some gin makers buy neutral spirits wholesale, and some distill their own. I learned that this can be, in addition to a matter of taste, a point of pride or disdain.

One gin representative emphasized that a "neutral spirit is a neutral spirit is a neutral spirit," so why not streamline the production process (and presumably reduce costs) by purchasing those neutral spirits wholesale instead of creating them from scratch? The logic is that gin's flavor magic happens with the special blend of botanicals, regardless of the neutral spirit's source.

Another gin representative expressed a patronizing disgust at this idea while showing me where the grains for his neutral spirits were sourced locally and delivered. As I peered into the fermentation vat, he emphasized quality control and pride of craft from start to finish.

Neutral spirit sourcing is just one aspect of how gin polarizes people, and like any definition relying on a negative and defining the spirit by what it is not—again, nonfiction, nondenominational, noncommittal, nonprofit—for a seemingly simple product, it very often confounds more than it clarifies.

Remember the distiller I spoke to? The man whose oak barrel aging and honey color made his juniper-based product a whiskey, technically speaking, and not a gin at all?

"We settled on barrel rested," he said.

6 THE GREAT STYLE DIVIDE

"Puss, give me two pennyworth of gin!"
I instantly put my mouth to the tube
and bid them receive it from the pipe under her paw.

FROM *THE LIFE AND UNCOMMON ADVENTURES OF CAPTAIN DUDLEY BRADSTREET* (1755)

If gin is categorized via a single class (juniper flavor) and three basic types that describe how juniper flavor is added (distilled, re-distilled, or compounded), why does Hendricks taste so different from Gordon's? Why do some gins promote the juniper flavor and some avoid it?

Enter gin styles.

Style differs from type and is not regulated by the TTB or defined in the BAM. Style is more of a gentleman's agreement, but "agreement" is not entirely accurate. And some styles are very, very precise. I learned that people can get very particular about gin style.

As gin evolved, its style evolution included controversy—how the juniper flavor is incorporated and to what degree the juniper flavor is tasted. Like the divide between companies who purchase neutral spirits and believe gin's magic happens in the botanical mix versus companies who distill their own neutral spirit and insist that juniper be the only flavor tasted in the product, gin style is exceptionally polarizing.

Each style tastes, smells, and frequently looks very different. The World Gin Awards honor competitors in ten different style categories. Among these style categories are some of the most popular and recognizable:

London Dry Gin

In lay terms, when a bottle is opened, and the pine scent hits hard and fast, it is likely a London Dry Gin. London Dry Gin relies on juniper, and juniper only, for its flavor. Unlike other styles with regional names, London Dry Gin does not have to be made in London, and common brands include Gordon's and Tanqueray.

To be a true London Dry Gin, absolutely nothing (no other botanical) is added after its distillation. London Dry Gin is also how many people first experience gin, and this style is typically very dry, heavily juniper flavored, and aromatic. These gins usually set the standard for taste comparison, and for many purists represent the one and only true gin taste.

Genever

While certainly the most recognized, London Dry Gin is not the oldest style of gin. That would likely be genever—although there is debate in some circles about whether genever is a style of gin, or gin is a style of genever. Genever, we learned, is the grandfather of modern gin, but for many gin enthusiasts, genever is an entirely different product.

This is another example of the proverbial rabbit hole and proof that gin is a confounding beverage. Genever differs in color and taste from London Dry Gin because genever is made from a malt grain base—typically, a mash of malted barley, rice, and corn. These malted grains give genever a darker color and mellower flavor—similar to a light-bodied whiskey. Unlike most gins, genever frequently spends time in barrels before making it to the market.

Bols, Rutte, and Fillier's are three widely recognized brands of genever.

Old Tom (and the First Vending Machine)

Often described as a mid-point between the sharp and precise London Dry Gin and the mellower genever, the Old Tom–style tastes much less arid than London Dry Gin, but it still carries a juniper punch. Old Tom developed in the years before the column still was perfected and neutral spirits were far from neutral tasting. Old Tom added sugar to temper the harsh alcohol taste, and this sweetness made it accessible and very popular.

The origin of Old Tom's name continues to be debated, but one certainty is its association with the first vending machine. In the mid-1700s, British Captain Dudley Bradstreet pioneered the process of selling cupfuls (or mouthfuls) of gin by pouring it down a lead pipe that dispensed under a sign illustrated with a cat's paw or mouth. This covert method was meant to avoid London's strict gin production and sales regulations.

Patrons would walk London's alleys, look for a black cat sign, and then either meow or call out "puss, puss" while placing money in a slot or nearby window. Although Bradstreet began the trend of these "Puss and Mew" houses featuring a black cat icon, there is little evidence linking him to the origin of "Old Tom" itself.

Stanley Clisby Arthur claims in his book, *Famous New Orleans Drinks and How to Mix 'Em*, that Old Tom acquired its name when a cat fell into a vat of gin, and Arthur is not the only person to cite this legend. The story has been repeated for so often that two modern gin sellers told it to me personally as fact.

Ginfoundry.com explains that a more credible origin story happened in the 1830s when Thomas Norris labeled his gin Old Tom, named after his former mentor Thomas Chamberlain, or "Old Tom." This style (Old Tom

FIGURE 3 Replica of circa 1755 Old Tom "Puss and Mew" sign. Courtesy of Beefeater Distillery Visitor Centre.

Chamberlain's style) is likely to have been taken on by Boord's of London who used both the name and the cat icon on their bottle. As Boord's was a popular gin brand at the time, the name stuck. Joseph Boord was the first distiller to register the image of a cat in his 1849 trademark for Old Tom Gin, which is thought to be the earliest registered trademark for any gin, so that gives this origin story particular credence.

Contemporary

Which brings us to the most contentious style: Contemporary. Also called New American, American, New World, and Western Dry, among others, these are all basic terms that capture styles of gin beginning, roughly, in the 1990s. While juniper is present, the flavor in these styles relies, often predominantly and overwhelmingly, on other botanicals. Hendricks, with its cucumber and rose flavors, is an example of this style.

When this type of evolution happens, in any area, there is often resistance. And that resistance very often plays out in unpleasant ways. Contemporary or New American is taken as a compliment in some gin circles—and in others, the worst kind of insult.

One gin merchant told me, "We are making gins that don't taste like traditional gin. I can get people to love gin when they taste this."

Another, firmly in the opposite corner, "We make gin the way gin is supposed to taste."

Not only is gin itself a polarizing beverage among consumers, but within the gin-making world, style is even more so.

NOTE FOR SIDEBAR:

Regarding Old Tom and the Puss and Mew shops, Dudley Bradstreet writes in 1755 that he "purchased in Moorfields the Sign of a Cat, and had it nailed to a Street Window; I then cause a Leaden Pipe, the small End out about an Inch, to be placed under the Paw of the Cat; the End that was within had a Funnel to it."

He continues to describe the success of his new invention: "at last I heard the Chink of Money, and a comfortable Voice say, 'Puss, give me two Pennyworth of Gin.' I instantly put my Mouth to the Tube, and bid them receive it from the Pipe under her Paw, and then measured and poured it into the Funnel, from whence they soon received it. Before Nigh I took six Shillings, the next Day above thirty Shillings, and afterwards three or four Pounds a Day."

NOTE FOR SIDEBAR: PLYMOUTH GIN

There are geographical, or location-specific, styles of gin. Notably, Plymouth Gin.

For many years, Plymouth Gin was location-specific to Plymouth, England. Labels might say "Plymouth-style" as a workaround, but if a gin was labeled as Plymouth Gin, it was made in Plymouth and nowhere else.

Interestingly, the original Plymouth Distillery building's proximity to the Royal William Victualling Yard (once a key aspect of the British Department of Defense) made it ideal for supplying the Navy with gin. It is one reason for the rapid rise of gin's British identity.

NOTE FOR SIDEBAR:

According to their website, the Bols family began producing liqueurs in Amsterdam in 1575 and genever specifically in 1664, which makes Bols one of the oldest distilling companies in the world. Because of its location in Amsterdam (as well as one of the family member's major share of the British East India Trading Company in 1700), Bols was privy to new spices and botanicals and led the development and manufacture of genever throughout the seventeenth, eighteenth, and nineteenth centuries.

7 DUTCH COURAGE AND THE BRITISH NAVY

Despite the Arabic origin of distillation, the subsequent addition of juniper to these spirits in Italy and the Netherlands, the United States role in the massive commercial rise of New American styles, and Filipinos drinking more per capita than any other country, gin remains firmly linked to England and British identity.

How did gin evolve from a European region's effort to ease a bleak existence (or from a cottage medicinal effort by Italian monks, depending upon who you ask) into a billion-dollar phenomenon with immediate British cultural associations?

Two big reasons: a Dutch-born king and the British Navy.

In 1585, the Dutch were fighting the Spanish for independence, and when the British began to support the Dutch these British soldiers were introduced to the local genever, which they believed gave them a boost and competitive advantage in battle.

Although the phrase "Dutch Courage" as a British euphemism for gin was not widely used until the Victorian period, the concept likely started when British soldiers first developed a taste in 1585 as they integrated into the Dutch community. When the British returned home, they brought a taste for genever with them; at the same time, Flemish Protestants fleeing to England brought genever with them, and this helped establish British production.

However, it was, essentially, a Dutch-born king and a series of government regulations that increased British gin consumption and solidified its identity. This increase in consumption coincided with staggering levels of addiction and social decline with the hundred-year-long British Gin Craze, and the Gin Craze is a major reason why gin is so closely associated with British identity.

As we learned, distillation was relatively common throughout Europe by the Middle Ages but was uncommon in England compared to beer and ale production. By the end of the sixteenth century and into the seventeenth, some wealthy residents had private stills, but these were not meant for mass consumption. In 1638, Sir Theodore de Mayerne was tasked with regulating the sale of distilled spirits, and this is where a massive domestic monopoly began—with the creation of the Worshipful Company of Distillers. (This group exists today.)

The group received a Royal Charter that gave members a monopoly to distill spirits. They also set prices and controlled production. Prices were high at this point, and production was tightly regulated.

High prices meant distilled liquor was rarely consumed by the public beyond a medicinal dose, and only the wealthy had easy recreational access. The poor still got drunk, but they drank the much more abundant (and cheap) locally brewed beers and ales.

So, poor people drank beer and wine—and lots of it, considering the state of the London water supply and economic realities, while wealthy people distilled spirits privately, set prices, and controlled sales.

Gin was not a thing for the masses.

Yet.

At the same time, a social and religious divide was happening. Similar to the current sharp divisions between liberal and conservative ideology, people divided between Catholics and Protestants. King James II was Catholic, and loyalty to the king meant loyalty to all trappings of Catholic culture, to include an appreciation for imported European wine and French brandy.

This all changed in 1689 when Dutch-born William III became king, and his Parliament did two things: banned imports of French wines and spirits and canceled the domestic monopoly for distillation. These two decisions caused gin's worldwide commercial success, cemented gin's identity as distinctly British—and set into motion one of the greatest examples of mass social decline,

Here is how it went down.

Ten years prior to his ascension, the Dutch Protestant William of Orange married King James II's daughter Mary.

When James was overthrown with the help and support from wealthy Protestant landowners and businessmen, William became king. In exchange, the wealthy landowners who supported the coup wanted to advance their business interests, and these interests included deregulating the distillation process so anyone with access and ability could manufacture spirits from their grain crops.

While some historians argue that these new policies were meant to benefit the English people by empowering them to expand the use of produce, it is also true that the farms producing the grains were, largely, owned by the men who put William in power.

Among his first acts as king, William agreed to ban French brandy and wine imports. (The French king was his sworn enemy.) He also raised duties and taxes on beer and ale to support the war against France. Suddenly, wine became less available while beer and ale became very expensive. For the first time in British history, spirits were cheaper than beer and more accessible than wine.

Enter gin.

By then, it was home grown and home manufactured, quick to produce, and cheap. Farmers and landowners were, naturally, very excited because of the profit potential for gin. They were offered incentives, too. For instance, businessmen (always men) who distilled grains were excused from the shared practice and community expense of providing room and board for soldiers.

At the same time, everything Catholic—to include the now-forbidden French wines and brandy, while not necessarily considered treason, was no way to express patriotism, so British people demonstrated loyalty to the new reign by shunning all things with Catholic influence and embracing all things Protestant, and in William's case, Dutch.

This meant that in addition to being cheap and abundant, there was also social and political pressure to produce and consume gin. Gin became sort of patriotic.

Remember that gin is just neutral spirit made from any grain and flavored with juniper. It requires no aging process and is cheap and quick to manufacture, so to keep up with this new demand, the rise in gin production was astronomical—and fast. By 1721, approximately 25 percent of London residents were employed in production of approximately two million gallons of—tax-free—gin annually.

People drank and drank, and gin quickly became too much of a good thing. Used to drinking beer and ale from large-sized glasses, people continued this practice, drinking gin by the pint and tumbler.

According to British statistical abstracts, the annual consumption of gin in England in 1700 was 1.23 million gallons. By 1714, this rose to two million gallons. By 1735, 6.4 million gallons, and by 1751, seven million gallons.

This rapid eighteenth-century commercial rise is how gin became closely aligned with British identity in its earliest years. The sheer volume of consumption rivaled any other country, and as England colonized throughout the world, soldiers and sailors brought a taste for gin with them. The United Kingdom still exports more gin around the world than it does beef and beer, its two other distinctly British commodities.

It was a massive surprise then, when I learned that the biggest gin drinkers, per capita, are not British. Or American. Or European. Or Australian.

Sixty million cases of gin are sold worldwide each year now with the Philippines accounting for twenty-two million of them: this makes the Philippines, not England, the biggest gin-drinking country per capita. The most popular brand of gin for Filipinos is Ginebra San Miguel—which uses sugarcane as its base. If the Philippines is not the most immediate association with gin consumption and commerce, that is easily forgiven.

Gin likes to reinvent itself.

Still, gin and British identity are linked.

Again from Celine Bossart in Vinepair's "The Complete and Slightly Insane History of Gin in England,"

"During World War II, while the Germans were bombing London in the Blitz, they were also bombing Plymouth because of the large British Royal Navy base there," Robby Nelson of Plymouth Gin says. "Plymouth gin was so beloved by the Navy that, when the fleet was notified that Plymouth had been bombed, one sailor said, 'Well, Hitler just lost the war!'"

Such was the esteem the English had for gin at the time. "Bombing London was bad enough, but attacking the home of the navy AND their gin was completely unacceptable," Nelson says.

In addition to bringing genever to England, the British Royal Navy receives credit for creating two popular gin-based cocktails, too—the Gin and Tonic and the Gimlet. British sailors were traveling to destinations with malaria outbreaks, and quinine was rationed to fight the disease. Quinine was effective, but it tasted foul. Simultaneously, the Schweppes company developed a carbonated soft drink that we now appreciate as tonic water. In addition to settling seasick stomachs, it tempered the quinine taste, but Quinine and Tonics never really caught on.

However, gin was also packed for these sea voyages, for its popularity and its practicality. (A bottle of gin better withstood cargo temperature fluctuations than, say, a bottle of wine.) Conveniently, vitamin C–rich limes were also rationed to prevent scurvy (and responsible for the "Limey" nickname).

These elements combined onboard to create a version of the modern Gin and Tonic, and sailors drank them liberally. Because their rationed limes were often preserved in the form of a cordial, these same British sailors also devised an onboard version of the Gimlet.

By region, the European Union is "by far the biggest destination for UK gin," with sales worth almost £290 million, up 14 percent in 2017, according to the Wine and Spirit Trade Association (WSTA), a group that represents more than 300 companies producing, importing, exporting, transporting and selling wines and spirits in the United Kingdom. In 2018, the WSTA stated that domestic sales of UK reached £1.9 billion.

WSTA chief executive Miles Beale is quoted with, "The global thirst for British gin shows no sign of slowing and there is no doubt that those overseas are drawn to the quality of gin made here in the UK Gin is a quintessentially British spirit, and perfect for anyone looking to tap into Brand Britain overseas."

NOTE FOR SIDEBAR:

The shift of liquor from medicine to social pastime, particularly in England, began as early as 1572 with England's strong water stores. According to research at distillerytrail.com, these new establishments helped transform social drinking habits away from low alcohol content beverages such as wine and ale into high alcohol distillates. "Up to this point, Londoners only imbibed distillates in the form of rudimentary tonics and tinctures produced by groups such as the Worshipful Company of Barbers, where patrons could receive a haircut, some bloodletting and a spirituous dram, all in the one sitting."

NOTE FOR SIDEBAR:

Pimm's No. 1 is a British, gin-based liqueur that is a key player in the classic British summertime cocktail, the Pimm's Cup. Popular at polo matches and tennis tournaments (an estimated 80,000 pints of Pimm's are sold at Wimbledon), the Pimm's Cup has now transitioned to a New Orleans favorite.

Pimm's Fruit Cup

- 1.5 cups Pimm's No. 1
- 1 orange, sliced thin
- 1 lemon, sliced thin
- 1 apple, sliced thin
- 3/4 cup mint leaves
- 1 1/2 cups ginger ale or lemon/lime soda
- 1 cucumber, cut lengthwise into wedges
- Ice

In a large pitcher, combine the Pimm's, fruit slices, and mint. Chill for about 10 minutes. Stir in the ginger ale. Put two cucumber wedges, standing on end, into a glass and fill halfway with ice. Pour the Pimm's mixture over the ice.

8 THE BRITISH GIN CRAZE

In the late 1600s, in the years surrounding the rise of William III and the 1689 de-regulation, if you were poor in England, or conversely, if you had money, you likely headed to London. Farm-based life in the country was hard, backbreaking work for little profit. Cities like London promised service jobs, trades, and better advancement opportunities for the poor—as well as rudimentary social safety nets for the indigent and infirm. For the wealthy, London offered politics, education, and entertainment. London was, during this phase of gin's rise, the social, political, and artistic center of England.

London population records at the time indicate two important statistics: a high concentration of people living in very close quarters and a sharp economic divide between the wealthy and the poor. Still, more and more people continued to crowd into London.

For the most part, this influx of people lived in poverty, and urban poverty meant inconsistent access to adequate food, clean water, and sanitation. Poverty was viewed then, as it is often viewed now (at least, by many with political power) as a moral failing among a lesser class of people. It was also a punishable offense, and social reformers, largely led by religious factions, blamed gin.

Why? Because much like those initial agrarian Low Country communities credited with developing a sort of genever by adding juniper to brandewijn as a means of coping with a hard, short life expectancy in a harsh climate, poor London residents also drank gin to blunt the edges of their realities.

Poor people drank a lot of gin in London.

Crime and mortality rates increased in tandem with this uptick in gin consumption, and these increases began nearly a century of gin-focused social decline, lawlessness, addiction, death—and failed attempts to address the issues. It became a familiar chicken-and-egg scenario. Depending upon perspective, gin either caused these social problems directly or became an indirect way of coping with them.

Gin was sometimes served warm as a restorative to ease the winter chill, and because it was cheap and abundant, families got drunk together for pennies. Given the polluted water supply options in the London slums, gin must have seemed practically nutritious.

Within a span of fifty years, London was producing 20 million gallons of gin. (This represents just the legal numbers.) People, including children, drank gin regularly. They drank gin, became addicted, got sick, and then they died. By many accounts, the death rate in London was higher than the birth rate for ten years, from 1723 to 1732. While troubling, high mortality rates were generally common for this era. Not as common were the gin-based reasons: hospitals and hospices were packed with "increasing multitudes of dropsical and consumptive people arising from the effects of spirituous liquors."

The man who paved the way for gin's rise—William III—died in 1702, and during the twenty-five years following his death, England was ruled by relatively short-term monarchs. Between gin's deregulation in 1689 and what would become the lengthy reign of King George II in 1727, Parliament largely controlled policy-making—which meant these lawmakers also controlled the gin. Since Parliament was strongly divided along political, social, and religious lines, this also meant bickering and a long period of inconsistency.

People in power failed to prioritize the initial gin crisis, and those who did address it failed to enact effective legislation. Alcohol addiction was considered a defect of character or moral failing of the lower class, so it was easy to compartmentalize and dismiss the situation.

Plus, in some wealthy class circles, there was a rationale that a bit of addiction might be a positive thing. In economic terms, it is called poverty theory, and the gist is that when workers remain dependent upon their employers, it assures a consistent (and cheap) workforce, so overall goods and services will prosper. Meaning, one easy way for the rich to remain rich was to keep the working class dependent—on a job, or on gin, or on a job to pay for gin.

For years, those in power had zero incentive to change the situation, so it continued to get worse. Nine thousand children in London died of alcohol poisoning in 1751. Along with addiction and child mortality rates, London crime levels rose.

England had a problem, and eventually this mass addiction and social upheaval became too pervasive to ignore. With 7,044 licensed gin retailers in a city of 600,000 people in the 1700s, plus thousands more street peddlers and a thriving off-license market, a conservative estimate puts one gin dealer for every sixty residents. By 1749, there were 17,000 gin shops in London, which puts that number closer to one legal dealer for every thirty-five residents.

If you are thinking this sounds like a modern opioid crisis, you are correct. Was this fair? Maybe not. There is evidence that gin was not solely to blame for this social decline. Remember that England was stretched very thin with its turnover in leadership and competing demands on finances—and its massive territorial wars while the wealth gap expanded between the haves and the have nots.

Historians continue to debate whether the associated rise in crime was caused by or an effect of gin. Scholars track the rise in London crime along with the rise in gin consumption, and scholars also attribute the rise in crime to London's overcrowding and poor economic conditions.

Regardless, gin took most of the blame.

"Most of the Murders and Robberies lately committed," said the London Grand Jury in 1736, "have been laid and concentrated at Gin Shops."

Except, what to do? Nobody could agree. Religious leaders, politicians, and social reformers blamed gin, and they launched a series of Gin Acts designed to prohibit consumption. There were a total of eight Gin Acts between 1729 and 1751, each with varying levels of prohibition and intricacy. (And not much lasting success, given the country's production volume and addiction rates.)

These acts were well intended, but they ignored the underlying social causes of the unrest (poverty and overcrowding) and focused on criminalizing gin drinkers.

Enter the 1751 Gin Act, or the Tippling Act. The legislation was much more effective than the earlier iterations for many reasons, largely because this effort was more carefully designed to limit gin's production, sale, and quality. It became less punitive, and most importantly, it harnessed the support of popular opinion and celebrity endorsements.

By celebrities, I mean writers and artists. Henry Fielding, London magistrate and famous author (to include the novel *Tom Jones*), cited the vices of this "lower order of people" in his 1751 *Enquiry into the Causes of the Late Increase of Robbers*. This treatise blamed the poor for the uptick in crime.

Fielding explained that this "lower order" wanted luxury but lacked innate work ethic, so committed crimes to fund these luxuries. He also blamed drunkenness. It was an easy way to assign blame and ease consciences.

In conjunction with Fielding's scathing publication, the equally famous artist and satirist William Hogarth produced a popular series of etchings, *Gin Lane* and *Beer*

Street. It is a bit of flawed analogy, but these etchings, for the period, were a combination of comic strip, editorial, and social media meme. They also became an endorsement. What made Hogarth particularly effective were the satirical nuances in his material that appealed to the intellectual or politically active set, while still conveying the message as directly as possible to the illiterate set.

No stranger to moralizing through illustration, Hogarth did not rely on subtlety.

The print is accompanied by the following verse:

Gin, cursed Fiend, with Fury fraught,
Makes human Race a Prey.
It enters by a deadly Draught
And steal our Life away.

He continues:

Theft, Murder, Perjury.
Damned Cup! that on the Vitals preys
That liquid Fire contains,
Which Madness to the heart conveys,
And rolls it thro' the Veins.

Contrast the two images. While each image satirizes situations and alludes to real people and circumstances with contemporary specificity, the quick interpretation is

FIGURE 4 *Gin Lane*. William Hogarth. 1751. Courtesy of The Miriam and Ira D. Wallach Division of Art, Prints and Photographs: Print Collection, The New York Public Library. "Gin Lane" New York Public Library Digital Collections.

FIGURE 5 *Beer Street*. William Hogarth. 1751. Courtesy of The Miriam and Ira D. Wallach Division of Art, Prints and Photographs: Print Collection, The New York Public Library. "Beer Street" New York Public Library Digital Collections.

that *Beer Street* thrives while *Gin Lane* decays. Even with zero understanding of the political and social atmosphere, a viewer can clearly see that *Beer Street* is prosperous and bustling, full of art, abundant food, and lively people dressed in clean clothing who happily go about their respectable business on a bright, sunny day.

On *Gin Lane*, the sky darkens while a drunken, syphilitic prostitute drops a baby to its death as a lunatic impales another dead baby's head on a spike while beating himself with a set of bellows. People are depicted naked, diseased, wailing, dead—all while drinking gin.

Again, the message is not meant to be subtle.

With assistance from this version of a social media campaign, the 1751 Gin Act/Tippling Act was passed. One goal of this effort (and a key difference from earlier legislation) was to simply decrease consumer gin sales.

To do this, the Act doubled the price of a gin license and made licenses only available to hospitality establishments: inns and taverns. In addition, it provided immunity and—this is important—a cash incentive for anyone willing to report illegal distillers to the authorities.

The Tippling Act was effective, and in just one year legal gin production fell by one-third. Conveniently, the legislation was followed by a period of extraordinarily weak grain harvests. Fearing a famine, an effort was made to make any grain was used to make sure people had food to eat, and all grain-distilled gins were prohibited just a few years later.

These fundamentals of gin's history in Britain underscore the origin of gin's influence in the world.

It also gave the Americans something to think about.

Not long after the British Gin Craze, the United States declared its independence—but not its independence from gin.

NOTE FOR SIDEBAR:

Gin is responsible for the first sort-of professional police force in England. In addition to pushing forward the 1751 Gin Act, magistrate and author Henry Fielding organized a group of men to apprehend offenders. Prior to these "Bow Street Runners," England relied on private citizens and professional "thief-takers" to fight crime.

9 ICE HARVEST, AMERICAN STYLE

As England's social order was crumbling, the United States was building itself. With the British Gin Craze and its effects lingering, Americans were also a bit wary of the spirit—but not wary enough, according to some.

Mason Locke Weems, colloquially Parson Weems, capitalized on the fear of alcohol with *The Drunkard's Looking Glass*, published circa 1812. Weems studied theology in London and saw the effects of the Gin Craze before returning to his United States home where he became a prolific author and book agent. (His biography of George Washington is responsible for the, likely false and certainly embellished, cherry tree anecdote.) As a fan of dramatic storytelling, his message is meant to shock.

A toothless, unattractive, slovenly woman is holding a large jug of gin. It was meant to frighten men, particularly men who maintained households—or hoped to maintain households—with women.

Parson Weems understood the power of sensation, and in addition to dramatic soldier biographies and anti-liquor

FIGURE 6 Weems, Mason Locke. *The Drunkard's Looking Glass*. Circa 1812. Courtesy of Rabelais: Fine Books on Food & Drink.

screeds, he is also responsible for titles that include *God's Revenge Against Adultery* and *God's Revenge Against Murder*. *The Drunkard's Looking Glass* was written with a similar sensationalism.

Thankfully, Americans were undeterred.

There were no London-level concentrated urban centers in the young country, so it took gin a few decades to reach its height of social popularity. While gin was certainly sold and enjoyed in the United States in the 1700s, its popularity grew in the 1800s as a result of two humble things: ice access and the invention of the cocktail.

Since refrigeration was not an option, and the British climate was often chilly, gin was initially served room temperature, lukewarm, or even hot. Americans embraced warm gin, and Massachusetts residents in particular took it a step farther. Consider this excerpt from *Legends of Woburn*, published in 1892 by Parker L. Converse, where he describes an iron bartender's tool.

> Now this loggerhead, or Flip-Dog, as it was sometimes called, consisted of a piece of iron about two feet long, one end being quite thick, while the other dwindled down to a handle; such an article being a main spoke in the furniture of every such place in those days.

And what was this tool used for?

> It was used in making flip, which was a mixture of beer, spirit and sugar, into which the loggerhead, hot from the

fire, was thrust, heating the compound and causing a froth on top which usually ran over the sides of the mug.

Yes. Woburn residents apparently enjoyed a frothy mix of hot gin mixed with beer and sugar.

Accounts of warm gin taking the edge off cold and rainy winter weather are frequent, and for a person living in the early nineteenth century, the idea of ice cold gin was just silly. While this might sound unappetizing to contemporary gin lovers, several hot gin beverage recipes still exist.

However, weather in the United States varied more significantly than in the United Kingdom, and eventually people wanted cooler beverages, especially in the summer months. In this way, gin's popularity in the United States— particularly when served as a cocktail—is linked directly to the ability to harvest ice.

Ice harvesting was initially a skeptical new concept, but with time, the idea caught on. As ice harvesting (and ice cabinets in homes) became more prevalent and efficient, ice costs decreased, and luxuries like ice cream and cold beverages were accessible to the poorer and middle classes. This desire for cold beverages included alcohol, which included gin. By the late 1800s recipe books were being printed for the home cook, to include guides for cold gin-based beverages.

Glassware also evolved.

Designed for practicality in an era where access to ice was prized and limited, stemware meant a drink would stay cooler longer, not warmed by a drinker's cupped hand. Over time, all-purpose stemware evolved from glasses with smaller, rounded sides to more defined shapes. Goblets lengthened or widened to accommodate sparkling wine bubbles, and for gin cocktails, stems stretched while rims expanded because the longer stem kept cocktails cool while the wider mouth gave the botanicals room to breathe. Conveniently, the cone's base provided a stable resting place for a toothpick skewered with olives or other condiments.

When homes became electrified in the early 1900s, technology had advanced to include electric refrigeration. Gin was now served ice cold, and people did not turn back. Cocktails became accessible to all social classes, and bartending was a respected profession. Kitchen recipe books included cocktail instructions, and any well-stocked home was expected to have liquor staples on hand. These liquors included gin.

A Note about Temperance

As American alcohol consumption increased in general, British Gin Craze memories served as a historical warning, and the popularity of the temperance movement grew. Throughout the nineteenth century, these temperance organizations, largely organized and led by women, pushed for a total ban on alcohol consumption, and these bans used British history as a strategy guide. This meant local support, celebrity endorsements, and a grass-roots effort that focused on fear.

Temperance organizations worked on a local level to obtain support for state-sponsored ordinances and laws that, while often unenforced, grew rapidly in number. Prior to Prohibition, laws in thirty-three states curtailed the sale, manufacture, transportation, or consumption of liquor. Again, these laws were largely unenforced until 1919 when the Volstead Act was passed to give teeth to the temperance effort. Federal law enforcement suddenly had authority to confront liquor production.

Interestingly, instead of vilifying gin, the temperance effort prompted a certain intrigue for gin. Gin consumption remained illegal during Prohibition, but the American taste and market for gin did not decrease. Its acquisition was just pushed underground. A new era of smuggling, organized crime, and homemade small batch "bathtub gin" efforts developed. (While illegal to manufacture during Prohibition, imported gin could always be purchased at pharmacies for medicinal use.)

In many ways, this mimicked the experience of gin drinkers in eighteenth-century England—and much like British gin in the eighteenth century, this homemade bathtub gin had to be consumed with caution. Instead of turpentine to mimic gin's flavor, Prohibition-era gin was diluted with wood alcohol. Some estimates note that 50,000 people died from wood alcohol poisoning during Prohibition.

Still, people wanted gin, and many ambitious cocktail makers—at least, those with the means—moved to major

European cities to ride out the Prohibition era. Their influence, to include the cocktail's influence, is clear in the large number of new "American-style" bars and cafes that were opened in London and Paris during the early twentieth century.

"American-Style" meant cocktails, and cocktails meant gin.

Conveniently, at the time that ice was being introduced and stemware was evolving, a new type of still was being developed that could strip away the chemical burn and make a more neutral-tasting spirit. Old Tom–style gins, the most popular at this time, initially tempered the product with added sugar, but with advancement in column still technology, alcohol began to taste better without the need for sugar. And cocktails made alcohol taste even better.

The BAM lists cocktails in their own class, akin to spirits themselves, and this class of twenty official "Recognized Cocktails," includes three that incorporate gin: Gimlet, Martini, and Tom Collins. (It should also be noted that Sloe Gin is not gin. It is its own type, noted under the "Liqueur/ Cordial" class, made by infusing sloe berries—buckthorn fruit—into any neutral spirit.)

Although just three gin cocktails are recognized at the federal level, by 1951, the Bartenders' Guild had registered 7,000 distinct cocktails.

I mentioned the origin of the Gin and Tonic and the Gimlet (thank you, British Navy!), but the origin of the Martini and the Tom Collins are equally interesting.

First, the Tom Collins and the Great Tom Collins Hoax. Mark Mason and Septimus Winner published "Tom Collins is my Name" in 1874, a novelty song and riff on the Great Tom Collins Hoax.

What is the Great Tom Collins Hoax? In the late nineteenth century, it was a popular joke to tell a gullible friend that a man named Tom Collins was going from bar to bar and talking terrible trash about your gullible friend. The intent was to share a long list of nasty rumors spread by this loudmouth, crude Tom Collins, and get your friend as upset as possible. Your friend would, no doubt, deny any knowledge of a person named Tom Collins and wonder why he was spreading such vile rumors. Your job, and the joke, would be to convince the friend to go searching for this mysterious man.

Depending on who you ask, this—the foray from bar to bar—may be the origin of the classic gin cocktail, when an enterprising bartender began to offer a gin cocktail to the victims of the prank. However popular the prank then, it does not age well, and with hindsight, it is a jerky thing to do.

However, the song caught on.

The Martini, however, possesses four credible origin stories. One legend claims that a famous nineteenth-century bartender, Jerry Thomas, invented the cocktail. Thomas, a flamboyant showman who pioneered mixology and performance, wrote a book called *The Bartender's Guide*. The 1887 edition, published posthumously, includes a recipe for the gin-based Martinez cocktail. However, the Martinez with

FIGURE 7 Winner, Sep. Tom Collins is my name. Boner & Co., W. H., Philadelphia, monographic, 1874.

its sweet vermouth, bitters, and maraschino liqueur is very different from a modern Martini.

Still, many claim that a Martini cocktail evolved from an original Martinez cocktail and cite the town of Martinez, California as proof. According to legend, a prospector who had just struck gold requested a celebration beverage at a Martinez bar.

Another guess is the Martini was named in honor of the bartender at New York's Knickerbocker Hotel, Martini di Arma di Taggia, after he served a gin and vermouth cocktail to John D. Rockefeller.

My favorite suggestion is the simplest: the Martini was a contraction of Martini & Rossi, a popular brand of sweet vermouth produced in 1863. This makes the most logical sense, and I can easily imagine a patron ordering a gin and vermouth by requesting the brand itself with "A gin and Martini, please."

NOTE FOR SIDEBAR:

In the 1942 film, *Casablanca*, Humphrey Bogart's iconic line "Of all the gin joints in all the world, she walks into mine" is delivered in his bar, Rick's American Café. In addition to establishing a character's nationality, the idea of an "American Café" is a direct result of the Prohibition-era exodus from the United States.

NOTE FOR SIDEBAR:

French 75

- 1.5 ounces gin
- Half ounce lemon juice
- Quarter ounce simple syrup
- Champagne

Add gin, lemon juice and sugar syrup to a cocktail shaker. Fill with ice and shake. Strain into an empty champagne flute. Top with champagne.

While some historians disagree with the provenance, it is widely believed the French 75 is the namesake of a First World War–era 75-millimeter Howitzer field gun.

The drink was described as delivering a kick similar to the weapon's impact.

Hot Gin Toddy

- 1.5 ounces gin
- 1 to 2 tablespoons simple syrup
- Boiling water
- Orange slices

Mix gin and simple syrup in a mug, squeeze orange slices into mug, and top with boiling water.

10 GINCIDENTS

Gincindent, gindiscretion, and ginvincibility all cheekily refer to those embarrassing moments that result from an excess of gin consumption.

During the site visits in preparation for this book, visits that spanned the United States and included Canadian, Irish, and French locations, the general premise was the same for each. The distillery proper was either viewed up close or from a distance via a glass window. There was also a tutorial that varied in depth, content, and formality. During these tutorials, I learned about the mechanics of gin development—specifically, the differences and approaches to the type of grain, the mix of botanicals, and the stills themselves.

One distiller spoke about the merits of locally made machinery, another touted a German company's engineering brilliance, and another chose a copper version custom made in Portugal. The stills ranged in size and color and price and complexity.

I smelled the pungent mash and dipped a finger into liquid poured directly from a spout. Each experience differed in scope and appeal, but the unifying factor at each of the distilleries I toured was the "gincident."

At the completion of the tour—or sometimes at the beginning—I found myself in the tasting area. These ranged from full bar setups with extensive cocktail menus to tiny gift shop corners, but inevitably, my guide would offer a sample taste. Sometimes it was just the two of us, and sometimes I was part of a larger group. An obvious attempt to boost sales while providing a succinct method of comparing and contrasting different flavors of gin, most people on these tours were eager to taste the samples.

However, some people preferred not to, stepping back to put physical distance between themselves and the sample glasses.

"Oh," the guide laughed, as if they'd just thought of the clever phrase, "have you experienced a 'gincident?'"

The tour guides almost always charmed the audience, either via giggle or groan, with the clever play on language, and I did smile the first time I heard it. Eventually though, I made up a game where I tried to predict the moment it would happen. The phrase felt annoying in the harmless manner of corny, eye-rolling dad jokes, but this idea of a gincident got into my head, and I could not cease thinking about the idea of gin as an antecedent to moments of epic human failure.

Most of my own gincidents were small in scope. An occasional headache or an upset stomach felt like a fair trade for loving gin too much. But what about those with serious gin disdain? I queried my colleagues. What, I wondered, sparked the aversion? Was there a specific gin-related moment? Did gin prompt a particular failure that made a lifelong impact?

At one "learn about gin" tutorial hosted by a neighborhood bar, I posed these questions to four women who generously offered me an empty seat at their table. During the event, these women drank the full-sized, flavored gin cocktails with enthusiasm, but they sniffed the tasting-sized samples of straight gin with apprehension.

I watched as all four women feigned interest in the straight gin samples—sipping but politely pushing the tasting cups away. I used the tour guide "gincident" line, got a laugh, and heard stories. Then I started using the line on other colleagues and heard even more stories. Gincidents abounded, and people were very willing to share.

I heard about being locked inside public bathroom stalls, vomiting in ambulances, pumped stomachs, two-day hangovers, and at least one arrest. People spoke, almost universally, of how any gin scent now calls those moments back in sharp, technicolor detail. With 90 percent reliability, I watched the exact same negative microexpressions: pursed lips, a barely perceptible head shake, and neck and shoulder twitch.

One friend's worst hangover happened in Paris. After an evening of wine at Île de la Cité, he described progressing to the surrealist Café le Deux Magot and ending the evening dancing on tables at Hotel Ibis while drinking warm gin shots, making the next morning's photos of him touring Jim Morrison's grave hilarious because he looked like a pale ghost.

However entertaining, these felt like relatively low-stakes consequences, so I started researching big, bad gincidents, and discovered an overwhelming amount of criminal history that cites not just alcohol, but gin specifically, as an aggravating factor—or defense.

Once again, I found Britain's Eighteenth Century Gin Craze set the standard. Not only are the records vivid because gin was so pervasive, they cite gin specifically by name.

Probably the most widely cited violent gin-fueled crime is Judith Dufour. In 1734, Judith Dufour worked a menial factory job as a yarn twister. Two years earlier, she had given birth to an illegitimate daughter, Mary, who was placed into the earliest iteration of a social safety net system: the workhouse.

Not quite an orphanage and not quite a jail and not quite an asylum, workhouses offered locations that gave both temporary and permanent care and occupation to poor, infirm, or unwanted people of all ages. Family members retained some rights and access to children placed in these workhouses, and one day Judith Dufour took Mary out of the workhouse for a few hours. The court documents detail what happened next.

On Sunday Night we took the Child into the Fields, and stripp'd it, and ty'd a Linen Handkerchief hard about its Neck to keep it from crying, and then laid it in a Ditch. And after that, we went together, and sold the Coat and Stay for a Shilling, and the Petticoat and Stockings for a

Groat. We parted the Money, and join'd for a Quartern of Gin.

Judith Dufour, along with (and possibly coerced by) a female colleague noted only as Sukey, strangled two-year-old Mary, stripped her clothing to sell, and left her in a ditch. They split the money and spent it on gin.

Since the workhouse had recently provided new clothing for Mary, the cash value of these clothes was the presumed motive. Likely suffering from a mental illness, intellectual delays, addiction, or a combination, Judith Dufour killed her child for access to the new clothing that she sold for gin money. Dufour confessed and was subsequently tried and hanged.

This gincident was significant because it challenged the eighteenth-century image of women, specifically the capacity of women to abuse substances and commit violent crimes. Judith Dufour launched a tabloid circus and became a (literal, as Hogarth satirizes her image in *Gin Lane*) poster child for the evils of gin.

Similar to Judith Dufour and in the same time frame, Mary Estwick's gincident also involved the death of a young child. Unlike Judith Dufour, Mary Estwick was an elderly woman tasked with caring for a baby at home and, while drunk on gin, she dropped the baby to its death in a burning fireplace.

Mary Estwick came home on Tuesday last about two in the afternoon, quite intoxicated with Gin, sate down before the fire and, it is supposed, had the child on her lap, which fell out of it on the hearth, and the fire catched hold of the child's clothes and burnt it to death.

Mary Estwick's crime showed that these lapses were not limited to youthful folly or wild behavior. They could happen within the presumed safety of home, and that reality scared the general population.

It was sex, not death, that made Jane Andrews famous during the Gin Craze. While her boss was out of town, Andrews played hooky from her job as a housemaid to day drink some gin.

She shut up his doors and went to Kensington Towne to a Gin-shop she usually frequented.

According to the documents, this is where Jane pursued her love of musician soldiers, a sexy blue collar worker, and bi-sexuality.

And there found a drummer of the guards of her acquaintance, a chimney-sweeper, and a woman traveller.

She brought them back to her boss's empty house to party.

She invited this guest home to her master's house where they drank plentifully from ten in the morning until four in the afternoon.

Then the scene got frisky. According to the records,

> Jane Andrews proposed to the company that they, and
> she, should all go to bed together. And thereupon they
> shut up the doors and windows, and tho twas but four in
> the afternoon, they stript and went into one bed together.

Word got out, and authorities found the foursome.

While I would never endorse gin-fueled murder or death of children, I offer a hearty gin toast to the memory of Jane Andrews, a woman who just seemed born in the wrong era.

Incidents like Judith Dufour, Mary Estwick, and Jane Andrews were proof to social reformers that gin was corrosive to women as well as men, and nicknames like "Mother's Ruin" and "Cuckold's Comfort" drew specific moral lines from the beverage to the gin-fueled crimes of eighteenth-century women. (Note the contrast to the heroic "Dutch Courage" for men.)

Conversely, while women were arrested and hanged for their gincidents, men were often acquitted for theirs. Henry Fielding, again during his role as Magistrate, describes men

> charged with theft and robbery . . . who I am forced to
> confine . . . and when they have afterwards become sober,
> I have plainly observed . . . that the gin alone was the cause
> of the transgression.

This rationale was fairly common. While women's gin crimes were viewed as dangerous trends that needed swift action to deter others, men's gin crimes were weighed against their general character and track record. Although sensational, women's gin crimes were still relatively rare—and therefore more dangerous.

Men committed the most crimes in eighteenth-century England, gauged both by volume and severity, but their crimes became commonplace. Gin-fueled crimes committed by men, even the most serious, were often overlooked as anomalies excused by their drunkenness.

As far as violent British gincidents go, Judith Dufour tops the list, but less noteworthy gincidents happened much more frequently and throughout the world. With thanks to the Ghosts of DC website and courtesy of *The Washington Post* archives, I learned about the 1893 case of George H. Shorter. Shorter, an American laborer, bet his co-workers that he "could drink a quart of gin with one pull out of the bottle."

Before the money he had won could be turned over to him, he began gasping for breath, reeled, and then plunged heavily forward on his face.

Unable to be resuscitated, Shorter was taken to the Washington Asylum Hospital where he died the next day. Newspaper archives are full of stories like Shorter's: a dare, a bet, or a decision gone wrong and ending in an accidental death.

This type of deadly gincident happened, more often than not, to the poor or working class. From being sloshed into dirty cups for a penny to drunk by the bottle on a bet, to crafted into intricate and gastronomically complex cocktails, over time, gin became the beverage choice for wit and glamour.

As this reputation evolved, particularly among the wealthier or artistic elite, gincidents assumed a level of joie de vivre. As gin became a symbol of the modern, good life, gincidents—at least those in elite circles—became stories told less as a cautionary tale or noted in the newspaper's court pages, and more with a level of cheekiness. Socialites embraced this cocktail sophistication, among them Zelda Fitzgerald and Tallulah Bankhead.

I can easily imagine either of them, depending upon which story you believe, with a good measure of gin in their systems and pinning a sprig of mistletoe to the backside of their fancy dresses while attending high society holiday dances.

As gin got glamorous, it also got dangerous, especially during Prohibition. Gin—remember quick, cheap, and easy to produce—led the underground alcohol market and helped solidify gang culture. Although gin-motivated, I hesitate to put a gincident label on these mob crimes because they were less about isolated incidents that happened while drunk on gin and more about how career criminals used gin to extort and threaten communities. There is gin-fueled crime, and there is gin-fueled *organized crime*.

Neither single accidents nor incidents confined to the decision of a lone person, this was a group of people establishing a syndicate that leveraged gin production and sales for money and power.

But if not in the gincident category, then where? Gin gangsters? The Gin Mob? Those stories could (and have) filled volumes.

The six Genna brothers are a good example of gin's link to Chicago's gang development and, particularly, how easy it was for cottage operations to grow—and grow quickly—into a criminal dynasty. (And yes, I chose the Gennas as an example because their family name is a linguistic callback to genever.)

According to the Mob Museum, in the early 1920s family moonshiners like the Gennas used small home stills to produce 200-proof alcohol, cut it with water, and then added juniper oil as flavor. They also provided hundreds of Chicago's poorest families with similar small batch stills to make homemade liquor in their own kitchens. Because these families needed money, they complied.

The Gennas supplied the base ingredients, and they paid these families cash. They also oversaw the production, collected the alcohol, and then sold the cheap, nasty gin to speakeasies for a considerable profit. With these cottage industries—highly illegal at the time—came intimidation, extortion, violence, theft, and murder. As the money and stakes grew, so did the gang membership and rival turf wars.

Obviously, the backstory is much more complex and nuanced, but small-time gin production had unintended, violent, national consequences.

In between the sensational gin-soaked baby murders, gin-inspired criminal enterprises, dumb gin dares, and the ordinary next-day gin headaches, are the just plain weird gincidents. A newspaper scan of *The New York Times* archive yielded a description from the September 9, 1896 issue about a snake charming element going awry during an impromptu magic show. The magicians, apparently, were paid in gin.

Also, the tragic 1951 gincident when writer William S. Burroughs shot his wife, fellow Beat-Generation icon Joan Vollmer, while aiming for a gin glass positioned on her forehead. Drunk on gin at a party in Mexico, he missed the glass and killed his wife.

But for most gin drinkers, gincidents are low stakes: headaches, some embarrassing photos, or an ill-advised romance. When asked to describe a person who may have experienced a gincident, one distiller did not hesitate when he described the response.

"They smell it, and they back right up."

NOTE FOR SIDEBAR:

As of this writing, there is an annual celebration planned in Australia called Gincident. For more information, please visit: gincident.info.

NOTE FOR SIDEBAR:

In a particularly interesting (to legal scholars and trivia enthusiasts) development, gin was mentioned by nickname during *Northern Ireland v. Gallagher*, a 1963 criminal case that established the difference between a psychopath and an intoxicated person. Patrick Gallagher murdered his wife. He was known to be a psychopath, and he was also drunk at the time of the murder. The case established that Gallagher's psychopathy was not brought on by alcohol.

Lord Denning makes the argument in court.

"If a man, whilst sane and sober, forms an intention to kill and makes preparation for it, knowing it is a wrong thing to do, and then gets himself drunk so as to give himself Dutch courage to do the killing, and whilst drunk carries out his intention, he cannot rely on this self-induced drunkenness as a defense to a charge of murder, nor even reducing it to manslaughter."

Of all the liquor references to make, Lord Denning chooses gin.

11 PORTRAITURE AND VISUALS

From William Hogarth to Mad Men–era magazine advertisements, visual depictions of gin reflect public sentiment of the time. Glamour or Hell, gin is typically expressed as a binary presentation of either sin or virtue and not, as author John Steinbeck noted (in a different context), just something people do. With gin, there is rarely ambiguity.

Conduct an internet search for gin, or juniper, or any of the iconic gin-based cocktails, and hundreds of images pop up. Botanical renderings from ancient medical texts, tourism posters, magazine advertisements, and internet memes.

I mentioned the etchings by William Hogarth and Parson Weems earlier, and these men held very particular views about gin. Look closely at the people depicted, and you'll see the syphilis sores, a barber intent on suicide, and a baby impaled on a spike. This was, in fairness, Hogarth's reality. Weems learned from Hogarth's reality, and his *Drunkard's Looking Glass* puts a woman in what appears to be a state of decomposition holding a bottle marked "gin."

However, it was not just Hogarth or Pastor Weems. These types of prints, or their equivalents, turn up every time gin is vilified visually.

Note the depiction of Elizabeth Inchbald at her writing desk. In a dramatic shock to eighteenth-century feminine expectations, Inchbald ran away to London, made a name for herself as an actress, then playwright, then novelist, and then theater critic. To understand how the artist felt about Inchwald and, by extension, the creative work of a woman, just look at the bottle of gin on her desk—and how the dog (or cat) is squatting. This offense: a professional woman capitalizing on her creative talent and in doing so, diminishing the work of men. Gin must be involved.

In images, gin got a negative social reputation from the very beginning. Conversely, early gin bottle labels are exquisite in their design.

This precision in visual representation goes back to the earliest days of labeling.

Antiquarian bookseller Don Lindgren showed me a ledger with dozens of colorful and ornate labels for gin and other British spirits pasted into the pages. Pages upon pages of vivid and elaborate labels from 1850 to 1860.

During this period, unscrupulous merchants would flavor inferior gin products with sulfuric acid, wood alcohol, turpentine, or worse. In response, gin manufacturers began identifying their bottles with ornate and colorful labels. Since producing labels, particularly in multiple colors with intricate design features, was expensive, only authentic

FIGURE 8 I'll Tell You What! That Such Things Are We Must Allow, But Such Things Never Were Till Now, Wigstead, Henry, Delineator, England, E. Jackson, Circa 1790. Playwright Elizabeth Inchbald Writing Puffs At A Table With A Bottle Of Gin And The Writings Of Aristotle, Rochester, And Congreve As A Dog Defecates On A Paper On The Floor. The Title Refers To Two Of Inchbald's Plays.

manufacturers were able to afford the process. Generally speaking, he explained, a fancy label helped guarantee the product's authenticity.

In this case, a set of the authentic labels were kept in ledgers, and those customs agents responsible for exporting gin would refer to the set of sample labels to check against outbound shipments. In addition to authenticating the product, this allowed for proper taxes to be charged and, in effect, was an early form of quality control.

From there, imagery became a sales tool. The more visually appealing, the more likely to attract customers. As advertising evolved, gin's image included bottle shape and size. In fact, I learned that bottle shape is key to gin's marketing. Bottles must appeal to bartenders and also retail consumers. Gin bottles are often colored—likely green—to disguise any sediment that might fall to the bottom. Or gin bottles are clear to demonstrate the product's purity.

One distiller shared his frustration. "Nothing was quite right. We wanted it to fit easily on a bar shelf or in a refrigerator door, be easily grip-able with one hand, and stand out visually in a line of other gins. It also can't break easily." After testing many bottle types for a new gin line, he found luck with a Chinese company that manufactures glass bottles for olive oil.

Over time, these bottle shapes have become iconic. There is no mistaking the squat, round shape of a Hendricks bottle. The silhouette and color of a blue Bombay Sapphire or green Tanqueray bottle are equally unmistakable.

"It leaves you breathless." This was a slogan in 1960s vodka advertising featuring a languid and sensual Julie Newmar. The double-entendre is a not-so-subtle put-down of gin and its pungency.

Gin, on the other hand, was advertised as "The nose knows."

FIGURE 9 Collection, Liquor Labels. Charles Day, Custom House Agent (London). *'SPIRIT LABELS' [title from binding front board].* London, Circa 1850–60. Courtesy of Rabelais: Fine Books on Food & Drink.

FIGURE 10 Ranchman's London Dry Gin advertisement. Circa 1969.

FIGURE 11 Gordon's Gin advertisement referencing The African Queen. Circa 1951.

As gin's visual presence and identity evolved, it began to include subtle—and not so subtle—references.

Ten years after *Casablanca*, Humphrey Bogart would embrace gin again as the booze-loving Charles Allnut in the movie adaptation of *The African Queen*. Katherine Hepburn's missionary character, Rose Sayer, does not share this love for liquor and empties the entirety of Bogart's Gordon's gin supply. It remains one of the best examples of product placement in film.

12 LYRICS AND VERSE

Stay away from me 'cause I'm in my sin
If this place gets raided give me my gin
Don't try me nobody 'cause you will never win
I'll fight the army and navy, yes, me and my gin

EXCERPT FROM ORIGINAL "GIN HOUSE BLUES"

It is difficult to imagine a spirit with more lyrical longevity than gin. It spans genres, and I am hard-pressed to name another alcohol that possesses this universal presence. Country music is all about beer, whiskey—and gin. Rap music notes marijuana with frequency, as well as gin. Jazz is sometimes about cocaine, and all about gin and gin joints. Rock and roll, in all iterations, cites gin, so it is no surprise that the blues that inspired it also includes gin. Irish traditional? Gin. Folk? Gin. Foxtrots from the Victrola period and novelty songs, too? All gin. Punk? Gin. Pop and Disco? Gin and gin.

As long as gin has existed, there have been verses written—and then sung—about it. Literary poets use gin as a device and trope, allegory and euphemism. Unlike long-form prose literature where gin is associated with glamour and sophistication just as often as squalor and sin, in verse form gin is—with few exceptions—consistently written as a soundtrack to heartache, poverty, or at best and most hopeful, nostalgia.

There is reason for this. Gin's history, as we've learned, ranks among the bleakest, drunk by the poorest, and heralded by those in most pain throughout its history. There's a connection to be made about the economics and literacy of consumers, too. When it was cheap and easy to find—or illegal and dangerous to find—gin became emblematic of the poor, so the words written and sung appealed that marginalized audience.

Gin, with its perpetual efficiency, is a way to evoke hard times.

Gin in verse is, unlike other spirits, almost universally associated with pain. Mick Jagger sang about gin-soaked barroom queens in Memphis, rock and roll–style, with a sort of reverence—but it is in no way a compliment.

Blues singer Bessie Smith advised us in scratchy recordings to stay away when she was in her gin, equating gin to, literally, sin. Gene Simmons, in full KISS makeup, laments in a glam metal roar that when he is down and out, it is cold gin time again. Northern Ireland's Divine Comedy and American Tom Waits sing wildly different—but still sad—songs with the same "Gin-Soaked Boy" title.

Kid Rock sang "Cocaine and Gin," Reverend Horton Heat, "Gin and Tonic Blues," and The Magnetic Fields likened love to a bottle of gin. None of these are happy songs.

Even gin's namesakes incorporate pain and nostalgia in their lyrics. Consider the Gin Blossoms lead singer who, before taking his own life, gave us "Hey Jealousy," the 1990s ballad about a man with no place to go, relying on pity to convince a former love to take him back, if only for a night. Likewise, "Jennifer Juniper," the 1968 song written by Donovan Leitch and inspired by Jennifer Boyd (sister of Pattie Boyd who was married to then-Beatle George Harrison), notes Jennifer Juniper longing for what she lacks.

This type of lament occurs not just in contemporary verse but actually increases in tone throughout earlier history. The year 1873 had George Stevens credited with "Gin and Beer" that included the graphic "And the gin that moisten'd Jones was eat'in up his bones" lyrics.

At worst, gin is sin and decay in verse and at best a sad nod to loneliness.

As gin evolved, it moved from a means for the poor to find comfort and distraction and was for a while embraced (and restricted) by the wealthy. Although gin has toggled between classes for centuries, it is difficult to locate a happy song about gin sung by either the affluent or the indigent.

And these are just words that are sung.

Verse that is meant to be read, not sung, also links gin to marginalized groups and depression. 1960s poet Gwendolyn Brooks, the first African American to win the Pulitzer Prize, makes observations about the poverty and hazards, particularly to the African American community, in verse that incorporates gin.

Consider "We Real Cool/The Pool Players/Seven at the Golden Shovel."

In this poem, Brooks chooses gin, and the effect is powerful.

"We lurk late. We strike straight. We sing sin. We thin gin."

Even with zero history of gin as context, as a reader, I would know this is a poem about a place with zero opportunities. The words Brooks chooses for her full verse signal as much: left, lurk, strike, thin, die, and yes—gin.

Because gin is so closely associated with hard times, it is no surprise that for a long period in United States history gin remained prominent in the African American lyrical community. From Alice Walker's description of Shug Avery singing at Harpo's gin joint in *The Color Purple*, to Delta blues guitar legend Bukka White's "Good Gin Blues" that invites a friend in to share some good gin, African American songwriters have embraced gin and its effects.

Bessie Smith in the 1920s gave rise to Nina Simone in the 1960s, which established gin's popularity (again) as the beverage for the most poorly treated, which, over time—arguably—laid the foundation for prevalence in rap and hip-hop.

This includes Snoop Dogg's iconic 1990s anthem "Gin and Juice," where the protagonists are rolling down the streets smoking indo and sipping on gin and juice. This combination of gin and marijuana has caused them to be—sing it with me—laid back.

From Nina Simone to Snoop Dogg, Merle Haggard to KISS, the Bee Gees to Wiz Khalifa, gin embraces all genres and lyrical forms. If you are sad and want to sing about it, gin is your liquor. If you are sad and want to write some poems, try gin.

13 FILM AND LITERATURE

Once you start seeing gin and gin's influence in film and literature, it is impossible to un-see. Gin and its accoutrements exist everywhere. Gin serves as a prop and plot device, and it has a long history of product placement, too. Sometimes the gin appears in cocktail glasses, and sometimes the bottles themselves.

When movie stars pose or vamp with a cocktail, it was more often than not meant to contain a gin-based beverage. *Casablanca* and the James Bond series are two of the most overt with their Gordon's bottles and specific process instructions, but recall any glamorous scene—generally a party or seduction—and it is likely to include conical stemware. And this conical stemware was originally designed to accommodate gin.

Remember that the BAM lists twenty federally recognized cocktails; just three are gin-based, but there is significant overrepresentation of gin in film. While I hesitate to call it a trope, the Martini glass or liquor bottle has become a definite film prop, similar to the cigarette.

Here is where I explain that, for these purposes, I have grouped film and literature together. Many of gin's iconic films originated as classic books or stories, or evolved from them, and the lines get a bit blurred. My intention is to capture the gin reference itself, with full credit to the authors of the original texts, as well as any television or movie adaptation that helped popularize the reference. Sometimes the gin reference is tied closely to the creators, sometimes it is associated more with the actors.

Because I focus on the characters—in some cases, gin itself qualifies as a character—I will, periodically, move between the two if that motion best illustrates gin's impact whether they exist in words or in images or both.

Gin in film carries particular significance to me because I tasted gin for the first time in a movie theater—and during the same period delivered a high school essay assignment on the topic of *The Great Gatsby*. The assignment described plot devices, but as a teenager I had zero reference for gin's presence in the plot. I was sixteen, and the theater manager poured cocktails for me. I wanted to get a little drunk. I wanted an A grade on the assignment. I did not think too much more beyond than this.

If a director or author is doing it right, gin references are equally subtle.

Consider the often-quoted line from 1942's *Casablanca*. "Of all the gin joints in all the towns in all the world, she walks into mine." Humphrey Bogart's character is reflecting upon his ill-fated romance with Ingrid Bergman, but in this famous scene he drinks whiskey, not gin. In fact, other than the bar's name, Rick's American Cafe—an homage to the Prohibition-fueled upswing in American ex-patriots—the only specific gin beverage reference in the film is a French 75 cocktail (gin, mixed with champagne, lemon, and sugar) when Yvonne arrives with her new Nazi boyfriend. Still, it is the gin line that audiences remember. It is the gin line that became iconic.

Conversely, gin is also so common in iconic films that it can be easily overlooked. Many can cite the *Casablanca* line, but what about the multiple gin lines in *It's a Wonderful Life*? ("Boys and girls and music—why do they need gin?") For Humphrey Bogart, the gin line makes the scene famous, but for Jimmy Stewart? Forgettable.

In both the novella and the film version of Truman Capote's *Breakfast at Tiffany's*, Holly Golightly (played by Audrey Hepburn in 1961) is a hard-drinking character who frequently refers to Martinis and also popularizes the White Angel—one half gin and one half of vodka. "Two more, my darling Mr. Bell," she purrs.

Likewise, Dashiell Hammett had his characters Nick and Nora Charles drink Bronx Cocktails (basically, a Martini with orange juice) in *The Thin Man*. Raymond Chandler chose Gimlets for Philip Marlowe and Terry Lennox's conversation in *The Long Good-Bye* to set up the proclamation, "A real Gimlet is half gin and half Rose's Lime Juice and nothing else. It beats Martinis hollow."

Gimlets became, for a while, a film favorite.

All About Eve featured Gimlets by name with Bette Davis as aging actress Margo Channing navigating a dangerous social climber, as did spy caper *North by Northwest*'s Roger O. Thornhill, played by Cary Grant. Gimlets—three, since readers will remember it "is the thing to do"—also made an appearance in 1947's *The Macomber Affair*, based on Ernest Hemingway's *The Short Happy Life of Francis Macomber*.

The sheer volume of gin use is impressive.

John Steinbeck upgrades his character Doc's liquor preference from beer milkshakes in *Cannery Row* to the uniquely named gin cocktail, the Webster F. Street Layaway Plan (a Martini with chartreuse instead of vermouth) in the sequel, *Sweet Thursday*. Jerry Lewis transforms into suave, Dean Martin-esque Buddy Love in *The Nutty Professor* with an equally unique gin-based Alaskan Polar Bear Heater, an unholy mix of gin, vodka, brandy, scotch, vinegar, vermouth, citrus peel, and a cherry.

More recent filmgoers will likely remember that Bradley Cooper's Jackson Maine first orders gin on the rocks in the beginning scenes of the most recent version of *A Star is Born*, but what about the Pan-Galactic Gargle Blaster from *The Hitchhiker's Guide to the Galaxy* and its three cubes of Arcturan Mega-Gin?

Most unusual juxtaposition? I think that happens when Val Kilmer, playing Jim Morrison in *The Doors*, drinks a Ramos Gin Fizz (gin, egg white, half and half, lemon and lime juices, simple syrup, and seltzer) while Tennessee

Williams also has his characters drink the same in both *A Streetcar Named Desire* and *Cat on a Hot Tin Roof*. The Ramos Gin Fizz is featured, too, in 1947's *Dead Reckoning* when Lizbeth Scott's Coral Chandler approaches Humphrey Bogart's Rip Murdock as she grieves for her murdered husband and delivers one of the best/worst lines in film with "What do you do, go on singing songs and drinking Ramos Gin Fizzes?"

I tag Hunter S. Thompson with the most self-destructive gin reference—his Singapore Sling in *Fear and Loathing in Las Vegas*:

> "Twenty-four hours ago we were sitting in the Pogo Lounge of the Beverly Heights Hotel—in the patio section of course—drinking Singapore Slings with mezcal on the side, hiding from the brutish realities of this foul year of Our Lord . . ."

For the uninitiated, that's a mix of gin, cherry brandy, and Benedictine—with mezcal.

The most hilarious literary gin reference? When Maggie Smith's character in *Evil Under the Sun* offers Hercule Poirot a double-entendre four-item menu that includes two gin-based choices, a White Lady (gin, triple sec, lemon juice, and egg white), Sidecar, Mainbrace (gin, triple sec, and grapefruit juice), or Between the Sheets.

The most highbrow? Maybe Somerset Maugham's gin-based Million Dollar Cocktail (gin, vermouth, pineapple juice, grenadine, and egg white) in his short story, "The Letter."

Apocalyptic? George Orwell's Victory Gin in *1984*. With government-assigned vices of gin and cigarettes, Orwell's Winston does his best to escape the dystopian alter-world, but among the most apocalyptic consequences is that in the process of this government control, gin loses all pleasure.

Funniest? The frequent Tom Collins references Robert DeNiro makes in *Meet the Parents*. (This is not the first Tom Collins film connection for De Niro. Astute audiences will remember that Tom Collins is the name chosen for his character, Sam "Ace" Rothstein, to register his personal safety deposit box in the mafia film *Casino*.)

Weirdest? For me, that is Nathaniel Hawthorne, author of *The Scarlet Letter*. After the novel's publication, a letter by Hawthorne to his friend Zachariah Burchmore appeared in Boston's *Saturday Evening Gazette*, later re-printed in *The New York Times*. He had run out of liquor.

"If P. had been a man," Hawthorne wrote, "he would have sent me some gin, according to his promise."

Apparently, this was newsworthy.

Which brings us, at last, to the categories of *most famous* and the *most tragic* gin references in film and literature,

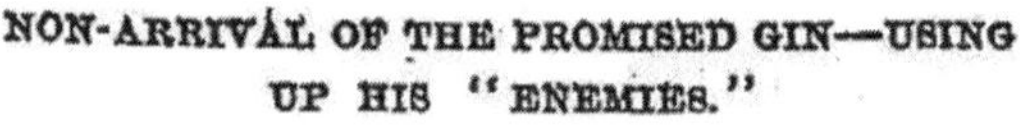

NON-ARRIVAL OF THE PROMISED GIN—USING UP HIS "ENEMIES."

FIGURE 12 *The New York Times*. 1850.

and for me, this is James Bond's Martini and Jay Gatsby's Gin Rickey. While Humphrey Bogart might claim the most iconic film line *about* gin, James Bond has the most famous reference to *gin itself.*

(I can argue that James Bond competes for the tragedy category, too, but not for the heartbreaking death of his love interest, Vesper Lynd who inspired his Vesper Martini. I nominate him for his role in killing the Martini with vodka.)

Shaken, not stirred. Growing up, I knew very little about Ian Fleming, but I knew "shaken, not stirred" delivered in a British accent commanded sophistication. I remember playground spy games with classmates and relaying this line with milk or juice at the cafeteria lunch table. The phrase has wedged itself into popular culture so tightly that even a devout teetotaler would place the reference. Except, the trajectory of the exact phrase gets complicated.

Although Ian Fleming has James Bond first say it aloud in 1958's novel *Dr. No*, and we hear the phrase in Bond's accented voice, it is the eponymous doctor who first says the words in the 1962 film version.

To pass the time during one particularly brutal Maine winter, my husband and I watched all the James Bond films, in order of release. Sean Connery, George Lazenby, Timothy Dalton, Pierce Brosnan, and Daniel Craig each order the gin beverage. Roger Moore is the only James Bond who does not. (They appear, but they are made for him in advance. By this film in the sequence, the in joke had already been established.)

It takes 1964's *Goldfinger* for Sean Connery's James Bond to say the phrase himself. From that point it becomes a signature, as well as a show of discernment that a palate could distinguish the difference.

And what is that difference? Both shaking and stirring are meant to chill and mix cocktails. Shaking makes the drink colder, quicker, and weaker while giving it a lighter and effervescent taste. Stirring keeps the original texture and makes the drink, while less cold, taste almost velvety. By shaking, James Bond is telling audiences that he prefers his Martinis icy and watered down.

He also liked them made with vodka, and many critics argue that vodka's presence in Bond films is one reason for its soaring popularity in the 1960s and 1970s.

Ian Fleming's Bond character is necessarily complex and mysterious, but Bond sometimes falls in love, too, as he did with Vesper Lynd, a double agent with a complex history of her own who ends her life in a tragic circumstance. Bond refers, however obliquely, to Vesper Lynd in the novels *Goldfinger, Diamonds are Forever, and On Her Majesty's Secret Service*, and in the films *Quantum of Solace* and *Spectre*, but it is *Casino Royale* that establishes the Vesper Martini.

Given her effect on him, Bond delivers one of his best lines in the 2006 film. Daniel Craig tells the bartender exactly how to make a Vesper Martini, in keeping with the novel. "Three measures of Gordon's, one of vodka, half a measure of Kina Lillet. Shake it over ice and add a thin slice of lemon peel." It mimics the book version, and when Craig is asked, somewhat cheekily as if the bartender is in on the cultural joke, if he'd like his Martini shaken or stirred, his answer is "Do I look like I give a damn?"

Although Bond helped make vodka popular, the Vesper Martini is another fantastic example of gin's product placement and effective product branding. Bond requests Gordon's gin, but in contrast, no specific vodka brand is named. This type of placement makes Gordon's become synonymous with all gin, and in doing so, it also affirms the London Dry Gin taste of Gordon's is the industry taste standard.

My personal favorite James Bond gin nod happens in *From Russia With Love*.

> Follow your fate, and be satisfied with it, and be glad not to be a second-hand motor salesman, or a yellow-press journalist, pickled in gin and nicotine, or a cripple—or dead.

Bottom line: Ian Fleming loved gin, and in loving gin his words cemented the beverage as the choice for masculine sophistication for generations. He also ruined it for generations with his taste for vodka because this taste for vodka established that a Martini could be made without gin. That, to me, makes James Bond's gin references the most famous in film.

Despite Bond's use of vodka in Martinis, my award for gin tragedy goes to F. Scott Fitzgerald's Gin Rickey (gin, lime juice, and soda water). Here is where I mention authors and how their personal preferences (and addictions) influence the characters they create. Reading James Bond novels, it is no surprise that Ian Fleming enjoyed gin. Thriller writer Patricia Highsmith was known to love Gin and Tonics, so her characters almost always do, too. It is the same for Ernest Hemingway and his love of Martinis. This is not uncommon. Writers write from life.

For Fitzgerald, however, the line between author and character is exceptionally blurred, and while he worked in fiction, the details from his life and his art were often undistinguishable. He and his wife Zelda Sayre (whose diaries he lifted heavily from) personified the Jazz Age lifestyle and its cocktail excess. Legend has it that Fitzgerald liked a Gin Rickey himself because the smell didn't linger on his breath.

By writing *The Great Gatsby*, what is often described as the great American novel and remains the publisher's most popular title, Fitzgerald made gin a tragic beverage and a pivotal plot point.

Although both Robert Redford and Leonardo DiCaprio hold champagne glasses in their film portrayals of the title character, gin is the star. Gin waits until chapter seven to appear, but its appearance is pivotal because it sets up the apartment party scene that leads to the book's tragic ending. Daisy asks her brute husband Tom to "make us a cold drink," and Tom returns with a tray of Gin Rickeys that "clicked full of ice."

Without these gin drinks, there would be no drunken truth telling, no drunk driving, and no deaths—either accidental or intentional. Without gin, there is no emotional reckoning. Gin is both the catalyst, and in some ways, the hero of the story.

As a longtime alcoholic, Fitzgerald's ailments included dyspnea, angina, coronary disease, and cardiomyopathy. He died from alcohol-related heart complications at age forty-four.

In a scene where his life mimicked his art, Fitzgerald—like Gatsby—had few funeral visitors. One of these visitors was author Dorothy Parker. Like the novel's character Owl-Eyes, who stands over Gatsby's coffin by accident, Parker allegedly stood over Fitzgerald's and whispered the same words.

"The poor son-of-a-bitch."

NOTES FOR SIDEBAR:

"I exercise strong self-control. I never drink anything stronger than gin before breakfast."

W. C. FIELDS

"The only time I ever enjoyed ironing was the day I accidentally got gin in the steam iron."

PHYLLIS DILLER

"Fortunately there is gin, the sole glimmer in this darkness. Do you feel the golden, copper-coloured light it kindles in you? I like walking through the city of an evening in the warmth of gin."

ALBERT CAMUS

"A lonely man is a lonesome thing, a stone, a bone, a stick, a receptacle for Gilbey's gin, a stooped figure sitting at the edge of a hotel bed, heaving copious sighs like the autumn wind."

JOHN CHEEVER

"There's truth in wine, and there may be some in gin and muddy beer; but whether it's truth worth my knowing, is another question."

GEORGE ELIOT

14 GINAISSANCE

During this book's research, I spent an afternoon in a gin tasting room that looked very much like any other sort of bar or tavern. Its central bar and cluster of tables prompted me to wonder about the distinction between bar, tavern, and tasting room. Was it to circumvent regulations in the way of private bottle clubs or the proper name for a space meant to promote a maker's products?

While I never received a definitive answer, it put me into a grammar and regulation headspace, and I vowed not to get sucked into architectural manuals and local liquor ordinances. Gin is sneaky though. One minute I was reading a clever menu and the next I had pulled up the history of the term "gin palace" on my phone.

This led to gin joints and gin houses. The earliest British gin establishments were small-scale operations, often unlicensed and because of this, hidden from view in the back rooms of a store or sitting room of a private home. Or, as we saw with the Old Tom sign, via clandestine vending machine and dark alley.

I learned that as women began drinking gin publicly in pace with men, the physical environment of the drinking establishments changed. Gas street lighting was introduced, and the process of manufacturing sheet glass and mirrors was perfected at this time, too. This meant drinking establishments could offer better lighting, longer operating hours, and more physical safety in addition to heightened decoration and glamour. Gin sellers capitalized on these developments and opened ornate, fancy spaces that appealed to this new market of women.

As gin's popularity grew and as these ornate, mirrored, highly stylized spaces proliferated, the idea of a "gin palace" was initially a slur meant to mock any garish new building. But these fancy gin palaces made it safer, more convenient, and appealing for women. This, in turn, made the spaces popular with men. One gin palace that catered to Manchester's factory workers in the mid-1830s was advertised to attract "not fewer than 2,000 persons, chiefly females" on a Saturday night.

Fearing another hours-long rabbit hole festooned with gin palace facts and gin joint legends, I turned my phone off to better absorb the atmosphere of my current gin-drinking establishment. There were no mirrors or gilded framing, no murals and no plush velvet. It was a minimalist approach to décor with natural light from big windows and smooth, polished chrome tables.

The lone bartender wore a gray knit beanie over long blonde curls, and he prepared gin beverages with an exaggerated flair, peeling lemon rind with a fancy zesting tool, one that made tiny spirals and intricate kinks with its channel knife. He coated glassware rims and interiors with liquids poured from apothecary-style glass bottles.

"To enhance the flavor," he explained as he slid the next cocktail toward me.

The crowd on this sunny afternoon skewed young—by young, I mean early twenties. It would be easy to point out the high-waisted denim pants, or the cropped tops, or the man buns as evidence of a hipster aesthetic attaching itself to gin. That would be the easy joke, but this particular group presented as contemporary, fashionable, and genuinely enthusiastic about their table of drinks. It looked, to me more than anything else like evidence of gin's popularity.

The number of women at their table was proportionate to the number of men, and occurred to me that, as a woman, just sitting in the public space was a fairly revolutionary act—and an act that I could, however indirectly, credit to gin. In addition to gin's role in creating the modern cocktail bar, I can argue that gin has a role in the rise of mixed-gender public drinking. Gin is one of the few spirits that directly appealed to women drinkers, both in its marketing and its prohibition.

I doubted anyone at the table knew about gin's role in their experience because why would they? That afternoon in the gin tasting room, the mixed-gender, stylish group clinked glasses in a toast, and it was such an ordinary gesture that I am certain they did not consider the evolution of their stemware as they touched rims in celebration, nor were they overtly affected by the linguist intricacies associated with their beverage.

They might have some opinion about gin style or a particular flavor profile. Maybe this group of friends knew about gin's role in modern film and literature beyond "shaken, not stirred," or "of all the gin joints," but maybe not. Maybe they understood the British Gin Craze or were grateful for ice cubes, but maybe not. If they watched Pope Francis deliver a TED talk and say that power is like drinking gin on an empty stomach, it was not a conversation topic I overheard.

I suspect they were drinking gin because it was fun, and at this point in time widely popular again. I suspect they ordered cocktail after cocktail because it was also effective. They were buying gin, enjoying the experience, and in doing so securing gin's role in contemporary conversation. In a way that is impossible to know in your early twenties—or from my experience as a teenager in a movie theater with a gin-filled Pepsi cup—they were enjoying their gin and carrying forward a long, time-honored tradition.

Cheers to that.

ACKNOWLEDGMENTS

Here is where I again emphasize that while I possess a measure of storytelling skill, I neither create gin, nor have I spent a lifetime studying it. It is the reading and collecting I enjoy. Like a magpie or crow, I look for the shiny bits.

Because of this, for the technical pieces, I drew heavily from the research and expertise of others: particularly Richard Barnett's *The Book of Gin* (Bloomsbury, 2016), Geraldine Coates's *Gin: The Essential Guide for Gin Aficionados* (Carlton Books, 2019), *Gin: A Global History* (Reaktion Books, 2012) by Lesley Jacobs Solmonson, and David T. Smith's *The Gin Dictionary* (Octopus Publishing Group, 2018). I recommend each of these books wholeheartedly, as well as the excellent websites: Gintime.com, Ginfoundry.com, Theginisin.com, Diffordsguide.com, Distillerytrail.com, Sipsmith.com, and Vinepair.com. Every gin question you have is likely contained in those resources, and while I noted this earlier, I want to emphasize it now. If you contact some of them as blindly as I did, they might offer the same kind responses.

My gin creator (and consumer) visits spanned the globe and included sites near and far away from my Maine home base: Dublin, Paris, Quebec City, New York, San Diego, Los Angeles, and Santa Cruz among them. Many gin makers contributed inspiration, content, or context, but my specific thanks include author Celine Bossart; Don Lindgren, owner of Rabelais: Fine Books on Food & Drink; Chris Dowe from Maine Distilleries; Ned Wight from New England Distilling; and Wes Moseman at Maine Craft Distilling. I also spent a particularly fun afternoon of samples at Round Turn Distilling, as well as an informative tutorial at The Maine House. Each of these people patiently answered my questions.

From a practical perspective, I thank Jessica Gilpatrick for her task-oriented encouragement, Joe Lombardo for his diner breakfast questions, and Tanya Whiton for her timely check-in and extreme editorial grace and talent.

And always, I thank my family—those by happy accident of birth and those by clear-eyed choice. Most of all, I thank Travis. To be living in recovery while watching his wife amass samples of gin and gin-related ephemera was, I assume, no easy task. But, as with everything, my husband offered a beautiful and pragmatic perspective.

"It wasn't hard for me at all," he said. "I was always a whiskey guy."

FIGURES

INDEX

Page references for illustrations appear in *italics*